D0149435

The Unwritten Rules of

BASEBALL

Also by Paul Dickson

BAT AND BALL BOOKS

The Dickson Baseball Dictionary (1989)

Baseball's Greatest Quotations (1991)

The Worth Book of Softball (1994)

The Joy of Keeping Score (1996)

Baseball: The Presidents' Game (1997)

The New Dickson Baseball Dictionary (1999)

The Hidden Language of Baseball (2003)

Baseball's Greatest Quotations, Revised Edition (2008)

BOOKS THAT ATTEMPT TO BRING ORDER TO A DISORDERLY UNIVERSE

The Official Rules (1979)

The Official Explanations (1980)

The New Official Rules (1989)

The Official Rules at Home (1996)

The Official Rules at Work (1996)

*The Official Rules for Lawyers, Politicians—
and Everyone They Torment (1996)*

The Official Rules for Golfers (1997)

The Official Rules and Explanations (1999)

The Official Rules of Life (2000)

The Etiquette,

Conventional Wisdom,

and Axiomatic Codes of

Our National Pastime

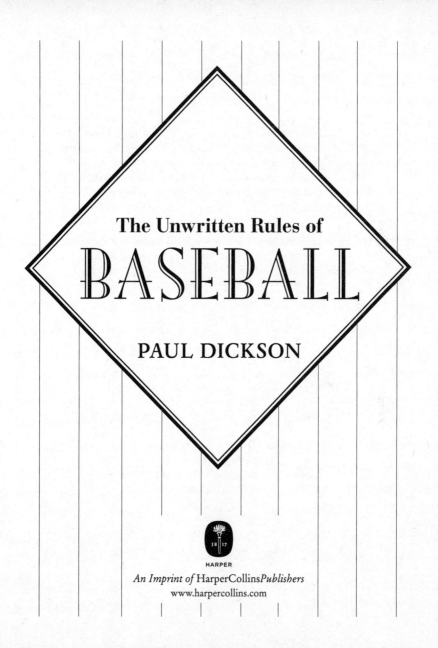

The Unwritten Rules of

BASEBALL

PAUL DICKSON

HARPER

An Imprint of HarperCollinsPublishers
www.harpercollins.com

HarperCollins books may be purchased for educational, business, or sales promotional use. For information, please e-mail the Special Markets Department at SPsales@harpercollins.com.

Designed by Ellen Cipriano

Library of Congress Cataloging-in-Publication Data
Dickson, Paul.
The unwritten rules of baseball / Paul Dickson. — 1st ed.
p. cm.
Includes bibliographical references.
ISBN 978-0-06-156105-4
1. Baseball. 2. Baseball—Miscellanea. I. Title.
GV867.D44 2009
796.357—dc22
2008015480

17 18 19   OV/RRD   20 19 18 17 16 15 14 13 12 11

To W. C. (Bill) Young for his dedication to this project and his many hours of advice and help.

Contents

Preface

Number one rule: attend to business.

—LEFTY GROVE

For some time now, I have been fascinated with the covert rather than the overt aspects of the game of baseball. I am not alone in this regard, as there are legions of fans and students of the game who have focused on the using of numbers to coax hidden verities from the game. These are the number crunchers of SABR (Society for American Baseball Research), who can tell you the probability of a double in Denver when the temperature is below 52°F or tell you the exact age at which the average batter or pitcher peaks.

But beyond the statistics, there are countless fascinating anthropological aspects of baseball. I am convinced that the game runs on a code of behavior, a set of beliefs and assumptions and practices that gives it both strength and character—and its own set of weaknesses. Nor is this code the exclusive domain of the men on the field while on the field—it extends with separate codes into the dugout and clubhouse, to the press box, and even into the stands.

This small book is an attempt to gather together all that I have learned from close to a hundred people—coaches, managers, players, old-timers, ardent fans, and writers—who have answered my questions, and from a fairly extensive examination of the baseball literature under the stewardship of Dave Kelly, the Library of Congress's designated sports authority. It is also an attempt to create a bookend of sorts for a man who saw his first game as a four-year-old and has been trying to get a handle on the game ever since.

The book is divided into two sections—the first on the unwritten rules themselves and the second on the axiomatic truths and mock-scientific laws that taken together constitute the conventional wisdom of the game.

PART I

The Unwritten Rules

Baseball is a game played with bat and
ball and governed by rules set forth by
a committee under the direction of the
commissioner of baseball. Baseball is
a game played by human beings and
governed by unwritten laws of survival
and self-preservation.

—JOE GARAGIOLA, *BASEBALL IS A*
FUNNY GAME

They have no sanction from the commissioner, appear no-where in any official publication, and are generally not posted on any clubhouse wall. The fans only hear about them from time to time, as weeks or months of the baseball season will go by with no word of them as they keep their normal low profile, until one is bent or broken and it becomes news for a few days.

Yet baseball's unofficial rules have a vitality and strength that passes from baseball generation to baseball generation. "The reason they are unwritten," Jeff Torborg told me when he managed the Florida Marlins, "is because you are sup-posed to be aware of what is professional and what is not."

These unwritten rules—or unwritten laws, as they are

sometimes called—represent a set of time-honored customs, rituals, and good manners that show a respect for the game, one's teammates, and one's opponent. They exist to provide a form of peaceful coexistence, allowing a diverse group of men on any given club to survive spring training, a 162-game schedule, and a possible postseason. "It's called 'The Gentlemen's Code,'" Colorado Rockies right fielder Brad Hawpe told Randy Holtz of the *Rocky Mountain News* in the wake of an unwritten rule violation in late May 2007, when Alex Rodriguez intentionally distracted a Toronto Blue Jays infielder trying to catch a pop-up. "It seems like baseball has more of those unwritten rules than any other sport because you play these teams so many times. When you play a team 18 times a year, you don't want to do something that's going to make them angry, because people remember stuff like that."

Philadelphia Phillies skipper Charlie Manuel sums it up differently: "They boil down to instructions for the way the game is supposed to be played." Pundit and baseball sage George F. Will has termed them "a generally understood etiquette." Yet the code is "elusive and fluid," according to Tim Keown, writing in *ESPN the Magazine* in 2001, "changing by the game, by the inning, by the pitch."

The unwritten rules as they exist today have to do with the rough-and-tumble game on the field in which players fight for an edge and take issue with disrespect as if they had just finished watching *The Godfather*.

Lest there be any question, there are penalties for violating these rules, and the penalties can be mentally or physically challenging. They range from getting publicly chastised in the media (which is now swelled by a twenty-four-hour sports news cycle and sports bloggers who hurl their own brand of nasty invective) to being benched or even traded or released. They can escalate to having the ball intentionally thrown at you by an opposing pitcher or having a base runner plow into you with the intention of bodily harm. The penalties are the means by which baseball polices itself.

Although they had existed for much longer, the unwritten laws were given a voice and a name by Joe Garagiola in 1960 in a primer he wrote with Martin Quigley on modern professional baseball, entitled *Baseball Is a Funny Game*. Despite the title, it was a dead-on serious book about the realities of the game of baseball as played between the foul lines. To Garagiola, they were laws of "survival and self-preservation." The game that Garagiola portrayed was a far cry from the game of boyhood dreams. "Now you have to win . . . There was never any place in your dreams for the knock-down pitch, the slide that breaks up the double play. But in the game that's real. Tip your hand that you don't like it, and you're through."

In the half century since Garagiola published his book, the unwritten rules have been widely discussed and codified on a number of occasions, most famously in 1986 when *Baseball Digest* published one of the best lists to ever appear about the game of baseball. "The Book of Unwritten Baseball Rules" was a collaborative effort and is quite comprehensive. It had originally appeared in the *Orange County Register* and was put together by Peter Schmuck, now of the *Baltimore Sun,* and Randy Youngman, who still writes for the *Register.* Today, their list appears on a number of baseball Web sites, introduced this way: "These are the rules that serious fans already know and new fans need to learn in order to speak baseball." Schmuck is quick to point out that they were put together in a few days and that there were more than the thirty on the original list.

Since then, there have been innumerable lists of such rules (*ESPN the Magazine, Sporting News, Time, Sports Illustrated,* and many daily newspapers) but none to match the 1986 list—which appears in its entirety as Appendix A at the back of this book (pages 225–227).

These unwritten rules also serve to give baseball its own style, which is much different than, say, pro football. Randy Galloway of the *Fort Worth Star-Telegram* has pointed to that rare two-sport athlete Deion Sanders to underscore the difference between the two games. His football side was "a Hollywood production, the ultimate in flash and self-adulation. But put him in a baseball uniform, and the transformation was amazing." Sanders was a walking testimony to the unwritten rules. Much the same could be said of Michael Jordan during his brief baseball career—a basketball persona versus a baseball one.

This is not to say that other sports and pursuits do not have unwritten rules with parallels to those in baseball. On January 12, 2005, the *Seattle Times* sports staff published separate sets of unwritten rules for baseball, basketball, football, golf, and hockey, and each began with the same basic rule: *Don't embarrass yourself, your teammates, or your opponent.*

To be sure, what many of these rules have in common seems to be a certain respect for the game and your opponent—to gain respect, give respect. In some instances, the unwritten rules have an added strategic benefit. In baseball, the benefit of the unwritten rules is that they keep the peace and allow players to concentrate on the game rather than some perceived breach of etiquette. A prime example in football is the unwritten rule that instructs the winning team to "take a knee"—that is, for the quarterback to receive the snap from the center and then fall to his knee, ending the play—in the final moments when the game has been decided. But thanks to a 1978 game known as the "Miracle of the Meadowlands," what seems like a tip of the cap to good sportsmanship also appears to be good strategy. The New York Giants led the Philadelphia Eagles and were running out the clock when quarterback Joe Pisarcik opted to hand off the football rather than end the play by taking a knee. He botched it. The ball bounced to the ground, and Eagles cornerback Herman Edwards picked it up and ran twenty-six yards for the winning touchdown.

In hockey, there are ritualistic rules for fighting that in many—but not all—cases are staged with the precision of ballet, while other times they take on the ferocity of a street fight with flashing blades. For the years he lorded over the sport, there was one inviolable unwritten rule, which was to keep your hands off Wayne Gretzky, the meal ticket for the struggling National Hockey League. *Sporting News* once reported that the unwritten rule stated that you were not even to give the Great One a dirty look.

Surfing—the serious form of the sport—is said to be all unwritten rules that surfers have developed over the years to determine who has the right to what wave. Rodeo is awash with unwritten rules for each event up through and including chuck wagon racing, which has its own set. ("Unwritten rules require the lead driver to move his team to the outside portion of the track, giving up the inside lane so that the other teams can catch up," according to one of the many Web sites about the event.) Rodeo is based on the code—real and imagined—of the cowboy, and without that element it would be less than the sum of its parts, rather than more.

NASCAR has an eighty-three-page rulebook, but an unwritten rule says that drivers will not pass after a caution flag comes out, which is a parallel notion to baseball's unwritten rule that says you don't steal bases with a huge lead. The parallel is even more complete when you realize that both of these old-school notions are thought by some people to be outmoded in the twenty-first century.

There are also stark contrasts in such matters as the unwritten rules for fan behavior. "When a batter steps to the plate to face a pitcher throwing 98-mph fastballs and 90-mph sliders near his head, fans must shout and clap and stomp their feet until the noise is loud enough to drown out Bill O'Reilly," writes Jim Caple, a senior writer for ESPN.com. When a golfer steps to the tee to hit a motionless golf ball, however, the gallery cannot whisper or so much as snap a photo.

Other rules transcend one sport and apply to other sports as well as life itself. One concerns new people coming to a team or organization and looks at the way they get along with an able, affable person on the staff who is not a fellow player or part of management—in baseball, a trainer, clubhouse man, or traveling secretary. The unwritten rule: "If he cannot get along with Joe, he probably doesn't belong here."

Careers are sometimes defined by a violation of an unwritten rule that may be recalled years after the offense was committed. For example, when the Baltimore Orioles invited switch-hitter Ben Davis to spring training in February 2008, he was identified as a man best remembered for breaking up Curt Schilling's perfect game on May 26, 2001, with a drag bunt in the eighth inning, which violated one of baseball's unwritten rules. Arizona held a 2–0 lead, so the bunt allowed the San Diego Padres to bring up the tying run. After the game, Diamondbacks manager Bob Brenly called Davis's decision "chicken," which is what is recalled today. "Davis was publicly humiliated and berated by fans and the media for weeks," wrote Derek Bolander on the popular Bleacher Report Web site on February 20, 2008. "He was said to have disrespected the game of baseball, and now his name will forever be linked to this incident." Forever is a long time to be in the unwritten rule purgatory, especially since there were those at the time who sided with Davis and the Padres. No less a baseball man than Joe Morgan summed it up best on

Sunday Night Baseball: "I never knew there was an unwritten rule saying you have to stop trying to win the ball game, no matter how good the pitcher is pitching."

Then there are the flamboyant home runs. San Francisco Giant Jeffrey Leonard, for instance, was still being cited more than twenty years after the fact as an example of a transgressor against the unwritten rule prohibiting showboat home runs for rounding the bases after hitting a homer with one arm hanging motionless at his side, which he called his "one flap down" trot. The flap down trot became a major point in the plot in the 1987 National League Championship Series because it so irritated the fans and the opposing St. Louis Cardinals that it was generally believed that it helped motivate them to win the series. "Aahh. Flap down Jeffrey," said Cardinals third-base coach Jose Oquendo to the Associated Press in 2002. Oquendo drove in the only run in Game 6 of that series and hit a three-run homer in Game 7 to send St. Louis to the World Series. "He didn't need to do that. But that fired us up. He didn't need to act like that going around the bases, but he did. And you see what happened," Oquendo said fifteen years after the fact.

Such incidents register not only in the memory of those who play the game and the enforcers in the media, but also with those who watch it. Watching a big-salaried player not

run out a grounder—even in spring training—puts a big as-
terisk on that player's name in the minds of the fans.

To be sure, there are those who are disdainful of these
"old-school" rules, and there are clubs that observe them less
strictly than others. Some old-timers tell you that there was
once a greater pressure to comply with the unwritten rules
and more upperclassmen to instruct you. "Six or seven big
guys cornering you in the locker room," recalls Angels batting coach and former major-league player Mickey Hatcher,
"and you learn your lessons pretty quickly."

Periodically, sports columnists and other observers of
the game declare that the "old- school" rules are doomed or
dying, making the argument that baseball is now a faster,
flashier game that should not be encumbered by the tradi-
tions of honor and gentlemanly anachronisms. For every
old-line newspaper columnist or sportscaster who sees the
unwritten rules as necessary to the good order of the game,
there are probably a dozen bloggers and Web-only columnists who decry them. "It's time to close the book on baseball's unwritten rules and enjoy this new baseball for what
it is. Crude, rude and in-your-face entertaining," says Steven
Schindler in his online baseball column. "And it is the new
age bigger, faster, stronger, harder-hitting Major League ballplayers that people pay their money to see. They fill today's

nostalgic retro ballparks to see football scores and 70 homers a season." Steve Czaban argues in his online sports column that the unwritten rules are supported by the baseball purists, whom he terms "the George Will-Keith Olbermann-Bob Costas-Ken Burns wing of our national pastime," but not by a broader fan base.

Others see something darker and more sinister about the unwritten rules. "I'm sorry, I can't let it go," opined Jerry Sullivan in the *Buffalo News* in 2001. "These unwritten rules of baseball are driving me insane. When you strip away the particulars, it really isn't about unwritten baseball rules. It's about the macho mentality, about foolish male pride. It's the same misguided impulse behind so much of the senseless violence nowadays—young males ready to fight over any perceived indignity, at any imagined slight." He adds that these outdated codes are passed along to the younger players and the next generation learns from the flat-screen TV in the living room. "So the next time you see a 12-year-old throw at another kid's head, don't be shocked. Chances are, he's probably just honoring the code."

Some baseball writers have commented about the decline of a significant number of the unwritten rules. Listen to *Albany Times Union* columnist Mark McGuire: "All unwritten rules regarding self-policing the game, humility, sportsmanship, team play and showing up an opponent are no longer operative. So stare down a pitcher who throws a belt-high pitch just inside the plate; use third-person in interviews (illustrating there is no 'I' in 'Team,' but there is a 'ME'); bunt to break up a no-hitter; try to go yard to left with a runner on second and no outs, and employ a home run trot slightly slower than a slug's transcontinental migration." He adds, alluding to one of the game's all-time retaliatory pitchers, "Nothing's gonna happen: Bob Gibson's retired."

Others insist the unwritten rules remain as constants that help to define the game. As ESPN's Tim Kurkjian has written, "What was good for Wagner, Cobb and Ruth is good for A-Rod and Ichiro."

Despite this, in the course of many face-to-face interviews I conducted during Florida and Arizona spring-training sessions in 2001 through 2003 and a number of follow-up interviews conducted by telephone and e-mail, I can report that the unwritten rules are alive and well. After spending considerable time thinking about the unwritten rules, I have come to my own conclusion, which is that they are neither archaic nor arcane, but simply exist. While some of the rules are immutable, others are open to interpretation and depend on circumstances. Over time, they have been modified, amended, and occasionally dropped. But they still exist and—for better or worse—give the game its essential character. The consensus seems to be that as long as there are veteran players, and coaches and managers who span baseball generations, the unwritten rules will be passed along. "The unsaid professionalism will always be there," commented Tony Muser when he managed the Kansas City Royals. Some teams are more determined than others to honor the unofficial rules. "The Yankees and Mariners are good examples," said broadcaster and former Toronto manager Buck Martinez. "They play hard and with respect."

A Short, Sordid History of
the Unwritten Rules

The concept of the "unwritten rule" is prehistoric and tribal.

But the term itself is a product of the eighteenth and nineteenth centuries. Such rules were posited as alternatives to written documents. They had early applications to the cloakrooms of Congress, the anterooms of the British Parliament, Army officers' quarters, Navy wardrooms, and, above all, the private male-only club. They were developed into codes and customs and fed by the mythology and parables of the nineteenth century in which the Knights of the Round Table rode forth from the fertile imagination of Sir Walter Scott espousing codes of revenge, honor, and retaliation.

The glue that held these groups together had as much

to do with the fact that men of power and influence had a right to say things to one another (no matter how candid) and make their own rules (no matter how exclusionary) with the expectation that their words and deeds would not become public. From this it was an easy leap to the offices of the officials and club owners in baseball where gentlemen's agreements and unwritten rules were made. Many of the customs and agreements at the basis of baseball began as unwritten and were later sanctioned by official agreements. The basic set of rules for staging the World Series, established in 1905 by New York Giants owner and president John T. Brush, were unofficial and unwritten at first. Many important features of these rules are still followed today, including the best-of-seven-games format. The Brush Rules also established the principle of a date after which no new players could be added to a team in anticipation of postseason play.

At another level, the concept moved from the lodge hall on Main Street to the baseball clubhouse, which still carries a nineteenth-century air to it. Other sports have locker rooms, but baseball and horse racing have, after all these years, clubhouses where unwritten rules often trump the written ones.

Exclusionary Code

The worst aspect of this code was that the unwritten rules were often vehicles for exclusion. Invisible lines could be drawn and bars erected. Those who created them could claim there was no such line or bar—nothing in writing. Take, for example, the unwritten rule that kept women off the field (save for an occasional pregame ceremony), which was in full force as late as 1957. During spring training that year, New York Yankee officials removed Laura Hendricks of the *St. Petersburg Times* from its dugout where she was covering a national telecast of the game and exiled her to a peephole position behind a backstop out of sight. Bob Fishel, head of Yankees public relations, explained to *Sporting News:* "Gosh! I hope she wasn't offended. It just isn't done. It's a general rule in the game that women are not allowed on the field. Partly, to protect them." The headline for this story in the March 6, 1957, *Sporting News* was "Fem Scribe Ejected from Field."

The unwritten baseball rule that was in force from the late nineteenth century to 1946 was the one that drew a color line to keep African-Americans from playing in organized baseball. As early as 1938, Major League Baseball commissioner Kenesaw Mountain Landis listened to a delegation of African-American leaders make an appeal for racial equality in baseball. Landis pointed out quite correctly that there was no rule in baseball keeping Negro players out of the game. As the late columnist Shirley Povich of the *Washington Post,* who had long crusaded for inclusion, put it: "No written rule, he implied. The unwritten rule they knew well."

Reporting on the event, Povich continues: "After hearing their plea, Landis said, 'Is that all, gentlemen?' 'Yes, it is, Commissioner,' the delegation leader said. 'Thank you for coming,' purred Landis. As the company filed out, Landis asked the club owners, 'What's next on the agenda?' One owner said: 'Wait a minute. Aren't we going to discuss the Negro question?' Landis said: 'There is nothing more to discuss. They asked to be heard, and we heard them.'"

This is how it always worked. There could be no discrimination because there was no written rule. In his autobiography *Veeck as in Wreck,* Bill Veeck reported that he tried to buy the bankrupt Philadelphia Phillies in 1943 and add black players to the roster, but owners rejected him—all the while insisting that there was no written prohibition against "Negroes" in the game.

This unwritten rule was finally broken on April 18, 1946,

when Jackie Robinson played for the Montreal Royals of the International League in preparation for a career with the Brooklyn Dodgers. In the major leagues, the rule was broken on April 15, 1947, when Robinson donned a Dodgers uniform. Today, conventional wisdom holds that the unwritten rule on the color bar fell in 1947 with Robinson, but it did not entirely. A new set of unwritten racial rules was imposed as black players were being examined for major-league rosters. These rules, which were in effect during the remainder of the 1940s and through the 1950s, were outlined by baseball historian Steve Treder in his study "The Persistent Color Line: Specific Instances of Racial Preference in Major League Player Evaluation Decisions after 1947," published in the 2001 edition of *Nine,* the journal of baseball history:

> A black player's Minor League statistics must be significantly better than a white player's for him to be given consideration for a Major League job. If a black player is given a chance at a Major League job, he will get just one shot with that organization. Unless he excels immediately, he will be discarded.
>
> The total number of black players on a team should be an even number so as to avoid dealing with the issue of asking a white player to be a black's roommate.

Whether the number of black players on any given team is even or odd, it must certainly be small.

As for the color bar itself, it was slow to be lifted in many places. In 1958, the AA Southern League was still prohibiting Negroes, which caused the end of the Dixie Series in 1959. The Boston Red Sox resisted until that same year—twelve years after Jackie Robinson broke the league's color barrier by joining the Brooklyn Dodgers—when they brought up infielder Pumpsie Green from the minors. The Yankees signed their first African-American player, Elston Howard, in 1955, the year after the crosstown Dodgers became the first team to field a majority of blacks in the starting lineup. On July, 17, 1954, against the Boston Braves, five of the nine Dodgers players who took the field were black, with Jim Gilliam at second base, Jackie Robinson at third, Sandy Amoros in left field, and a battery of Roy Campanella and Don Newcombe.

A more recent example of an unwritten rule based on prejudice is the one that held that a team with too many Latino names was not going to be a contender—that it would somehow gain a critical mass of men who seemed too happy-go-lucky to win. It stemmed from an era when only light-skinned players from Latin America were considered suitable to play in the majors and when they lived under strict rules about speaking "English only."

Tim Wendel, one of the founders of *USA Baseball Weekly* and a writer who has written extensively about Latino players (including his definitive work *The New Face of Baseball: The One-Hundred-Year Rise and Triumph of Latinos in America's Favorite Sport*), believes that this unwritten rule may have gathered momentum with the San Francisco Giants in the early 1960s, when the team never really made it despite the great talent of Latin players such as Juan Marichal, Orlando Cepeda, and the Alou brothers (Felipe, Jesus, and Matty). The team was managed by Alvin Dark, who came up with a policy of "English only" when players were in uniform. The closest that the team came to a total success was its loss in the 1962 World Series. The team that turned the unwritten rule on its head was the Pittsburgh Pirates, led by Latin stars such as Roberto Clemente and Manny Sanguillen, who bested the Baltimore Orioles in the 1971 World Series. The Pirates also became the first major-league team ever to start nine black players in a game.

Wendel believes that the unwritten rule was fostered by men like Dark who did not understand a subtle but significant difference in the Latin players, who are unlike those who are raised in an American culture of stoicism and silent despair when things go wrong. Strike out three times and you hang your head in shame and study your shoelaces, but Latino players who strike out three times come to their fourth at bat with a smile looking for a hit. "It's no accident that the term 'golden sombrero'—for a player who strikes out four times in a game—comes from Latino players." Wendel adds that Roberto Clemente was probably the most important figure in changing this notion—"the Latino Jackie Robinson."

Cheating as a Sacrament

The dark side of the unwritten rules may be a culture in which deception, silence, and cheating have the status of sacrament. Peter Schmuck, baseball columnist for the *Baltimore Sun* and coauthor of the classic 1986 enumeration of unwritten rules, wrote: "The culture that produced Gaylord Perry developed because baseball's rules are written in such a way that many forms of 'cheating' must be detected by the opponent instead of the umpire. If you miss a base, the other team has to appeal. If a pitcher is scuffing the ball, generally the opposing manager must bring it to the attention of the umpires. I believe this created an atmosphere where getting away with something was almost admired, which certainly could have led to the mindset that spawned the steroid mess."

Schmuck is not the only one to put the steroid mess on the debit side of the unwritten rules debate. At the time of the 2007 Mitchell Report, the written rules on drugs had been largely overlooked for more than a decade by players, owners, and the staff at the commissioner's office, all of whom seemed to be more serious about the unwritten rules about getting an edge and keeping clubhouse secrets than about obeying the written rules. More than one editorialist made the point that if Major League Baseball was as serious about the written rules as it was about the unwritten rules, there would have been much less of a problem.

1.0.0. The Unwritten Rules for Players–
the Basic Canon of Baseball Behavior

If there is a taxonomy to this list, it is that it works from moving the rules of the clubhouse—"The Code of the Clubhouse," in the words of author Ross Bernstein—onto the playing field.

1.1.0. The Clubhouse Is a Sanctuary

During spring training in 2002, the New York Yankees expelled Ruben Rivera for violating this rule. He had stolen Derek Jeter's glove and bat and was apparently ready to sell them to a dealer in sports memorabilia for $2,500. A few days later, Yankees manager Joe Torre explained why the penalty was so quick and so harsh: "To me it's very important that you trust the people you are playing alongside of. The clubhouse is very sacred. You spend more time in the clubhouse than you do in your home during the course of the season. The players should be able to escape the pressures of the day . . . the media, the game itself." He added: "Players are now like rock stars—they command a lot of attention. They need a place to get away from all that."

1.1.1. A Player's Locker Is Off Limits to Everyone Save for the Man Whose Name Appears on It

As Don Baylor, then managing the Colorado Rockies, told a reporter in 1998 after an incident in which a reporter had been seen poking around one of his player's lockers, "You don't go into a guy's locker. Even when I was a player, if another player asked for something and it was in my locker, no way. You don't do it."

1.1.2. This Sanctuary Rule Also Applies to the Visiting Team's Clubhouse

In 1990, Murray Chass of the *New York Times* wrote an article, "Bats in Bronx: A Yankee Caper," in which he said that New York Yankees front-office employees, under orders from George Steinbrenner, for several years had secretly checked the visiting team clubhouse late at night to see if the opposition's bats were altered. Frank Robinson, then managing the Baltimore Orioles, was among those expressing a strong negative reaction: "It's an unwritten rule, I have no right to do that. I would never go into another clubhouse here." The assumption, according to then Cleveland Indians manager John McNamara, was that a visiting clubhouse was your home "and that you don't expect people to come invading your privacy."

1.1.3. Don't Even Think about Visiting Your Opponent's Clubhouse for Any Reason Whatsoever

On April 3, 2002, Red Sox pitching ace Pedro Martinez took the opportunity of a rain delay to visit the Toronto Blue

Jays clubhouse at Fenway. Blue Jays manager Buck Martinez learned what had happened and angrily invoked the unwritten rule of fraternization as well as clubhouse sanctity. "I don't understand the mentality of a player being in another player's locker room," said the angry manager, who was just as mad at any of his own players who may have welcomed the pitcher, especially since the Red Sox ace had hit Shannon Stewart of the Blue Jays with a pitch in the previous game. "If I were Shannon Stewart I've got to think of taking a pop at him or something," said Martinez.

This transgression got a lot of media attention and the term "unwritten rule" was widely invoked, but that did not stop it from happening again. In September 2007, after former New York Met Julio Franco had signed with the Atlanta Braves, he wandered into the clubhouse of his former teammates to say hello, irking the Mets, most notably manager Willie Randolph and pitcher Tom Glavine. "That wouldn't go over too well in the clubhouses I grew up in," Randolph told the *Record* (Hackensack, New Jersey), to which Glavine added: "You play long enough, I guess you see everything."

1.2.0. Refrain from Criticizing a Teammate
or the Team in Public

"What you see here, what you say here, what you hear here, when you leave here let it stay here—that is still the rule," says Rick Dempsey, first-base coach of the Baltimore Orioles, quoting a time-honored clubhouse commandment.

Breaches of this rule are so few and far between that when they occur, they make headlines. In 1979, Dave Revering made headlines with a postseason assessment of the worst team in the history of the Oakland A's. "Our biggest problem is lack of talent. We have about five men who can play every day in the Major Leagues." Asked about his personal goals by Tom Weir of *Sporting News*, Revering replied, "To get out of here."

Violations of this rule are more serious when made during the season. In June 2002, San Francisco Giants outfielder Barry Bonds complained that his pitchers weren't retaliating when he was getting hit. Bonds's complaint had merit—Giants hitters had been hit with a pitch three times as often as Giants pitchers had hit opposing hitters up to that point in the season—but making it public was a clear violation of the clubhouse rule.

There is a version of this rule that extends through every

level of the game, including Little League, where the first rule of the baseball parent is that one does not criticize the behavior of the players—at least not within earshot of the fans.

1.2.1. Do Not Criticize a Teammate in Print

Jim Bouton broke this rule in his book *Ball Four,* and there are old-timers, Joe Torre among them, who more than thirty years later still bristle when this book is mentioned. When it was first published in 1970, Commissioner Bowie Kuhn decreed that it had "done the game a grave disservice" and summoned Bouton, who was then pitching for the Houston Astros, to his office for a dressing-down. Tame by today's standards, the book chronicles players taking amphetamines (or "greenies," as they were called in his day), going to great lengths to spy on women in various states of undress, and boorishly rejecting children seeking autographs.

Dick Young of the New York *Daily News* termed Bouton "a social leper." When Bouton showed up in 1970 to pitch in San Diego, he found a charred copy of the book in the visitors' locker room. When the Astros got to Cincinnati, Pete Rose stood on the top step of the dugout and bellowed "Fuck you, Shakespeare." And the anger persisted. According to *New*

York Times sportswriter Gerald Eskenazi, *Ball Four* "angered Mickey Mantle and Whitey Ford and Yogi Berra to such an extent that Bouton, a one-time twenty-game winner, wasn't invited to Yankee Old-Timers' games for more than thirty years, until the end of the 1990s."

This is not to say that Bouton was the only violator, but he still stands as the most prominent. And as if to underscore his position, Bouton brought out new editions in 1981, 1990, and 2000, and has written four other books.

The closest any subsequent baseball book has come to creating the same kind of outrage as *Ball Four* was with the publication in 2005 of Jose Canseco's *Juiced: Wild Times, Rampant 'Roids, Smash Hits, and How Baseball Got Big.* "Your tell-all book will sell, because it breaks the clubhouse's code of silence and violates an unwritten rule of the game. You aired the dirty laundry of your baseball brethren" is how pitcher Todd Jones reacted to Canseco's book.

1.2.2. Never Rat Out a Teammate

The headline-making violation of the ratting-out rule came in the wake of the Mitchell Report on the use of performance-enhancing drugs in baseball. During a congressional kangaroo court convened to assess the guilt of Roger Clemens, former teammate Andy Pettitte submitted testimony that was most damning for Clemens and his case for telling the truth. By being under oath, Pettitte had his own good reason for testifying against Clemens, but "inside baseball" he violated the commandment when he told congressional investigators that Clemens told him he used HGH nearly a decade ago. As many writers and bloggers reminded us in late winter 2008, rats are not highly regarded in any big-league clubhouse, even a player as popular with his teammates as Pettitte.

1.2.3. Never Rat Out a Former Teammate to an Umpire

When players change teams, they know stuff about their former teammates and the temptation is to pass that information along. "If that guy gets checked," pitcher Todd Jones wrote in a June 19, 2005, column in the *Birmingham News*, "expect retaliation." Jones was reacting to an incident on June 14, 2005, in Anaheim when Angels pitcher Brendan Donnelly was checked by the umpires before he threw a pitch and got ejected because they found pine tar on his glove. "Sounds like an inside job to me," Jones reacted. "Frank Robinson maybe was tipped off."

The logical suspect, known to all, was former Angel Jose Guillen, who had been traded by the Angels to the Washington Nationals, where Robinson managed.

1.3.0. Always Show Respect for
Your Teammates

When Boston's Pedro Martinez was taken out of the Opening Night game in Baltimore on April 8, 2004, he walked out of Camden Yards in the eighth inning, showing, as Hal Bodley termed it in *USA Today*, "little respect for his teammates." In Toronto in the 1980s, during one of his one-year stints as Yankees manager, the author watched manager Billy Martin go into the Yankees' dugout, put his civilian clothes on, and then walk back out through the dugout and down the sidelines and out of the park.

1.4.0. Respect the Superstitions and
Routines of Ballplayers

The level to which baseball players are superstitious is legendary. From the days of the old Baltimore Orioles, who drank turkey gravy before important games, jinxes and hoodoos have been observed and honored with a primitive religiosity. Some are individual, such as a manager wearing good-luck warm-up jackets through a heat spell (Tony La Russa), or a player getting rid of a bat after one hundred hits (Honus Wagner), or the need to eat chicken before each game (Wade Boggs). The game is awash in them. Then there are the general superstitions that seem to be observed by many players: tapping one's bat on the plate when coming to bat and/or making a mark in the batter's box with the head of the bat; not talking about the outcome of a seven-game series until it is over; not shaving until the team loses after the first win of the season; chewing only three wads of gum per game; or not "statting," which is to jinx a player by mentioning his excellent statistics.

1.4.1. Do NOT Mess with
Another Player's Clubhouse Superstitions

One does not ever question the validity of others' superstitions. The countless players who observe the time-honored superstition of not stepping on the foul line dare not say a negative word to teammates who observe the time-honored countersuperstition of stepping on the foul line. Ditto for the many players who step on second or third base when transitioning from the field to the dugout but respect teammates who avoid stepping on the bag.

The worst thing that can happen is when someone in uniform challenges a superstition. Mel Stottlemyre, the Yankees' longtime ace and current pitching coach, told Larry Stone of the *Seattle Times* how he came to believe in the power of foul-line avoidance. He said that a Yankees coach, Jim Hegan, told him one day before a game with the Twins that it was a silly belief, and that stepping on the foul line would have no effect on his performance. Stottlemyre thought he might have a point, and cavalierly stepped on the foul line as he went out to face the Twins.

Here's his own account of that day's game in *The Baseball Almanac:* "The first batter I faced was Ted Uhlaender, and he hit a line drive off my left shin. It went for a hit. [Rod] Carew, [Tony] Oliva and [Harmon] Killebrew followed with extra-base hits. The fifth man hit a single and scored and I was charged with five runs. I haven't stepped on a foul line since."

1.4.2. Ballplayers Have Routines That Are to Be Honored and Not Interrupted

Routines go beyond basic superstitions in that they represent a pattern of behavior that brings a sense of control to the ball-player. They are found at every level of the game, beginning with Little Leaguers, who soon learn that their luck seems to get better when they put their left shoe on first.

Pirates coach Rich Donnelly told anthropologist George Gmelch for his article "Baseball Magic" (in which he compared the rituals and routines of ballplayers to the fishermen of the Trobriand Islands studied by Bronislaw Malinowski between 1915 and 1918): "They're like trained animals. They come out here [to the ballpark] and every-thing has to be the same, they don't like anything that knocks them off their routine. Just look at the dugout and you'll see every guy sitting in the same spot every night. It's amazing, everybody in the same spot. And don't you dare take someone's seat. If a guy comes up from the minors and sits here, they'll say, 'Hey, Jim sits here, find an-other seat.' You watch the pitcher warm up and he'll do the same thing every time. And when you go on the road it's the same way. You've got a routine and you adhere to it and you don't want anybody knocking you off it" ("Superstition and Ritual in American Baseball," *Elysian Fields Quarterly* 11, no. 3 [1992]: pp. 25–36).

1.5.0. It Is the Pitcher's Job to Protect His Hitters and Enforce Many of the Unwritten Rules

In order to enforce the rules, the pitcher can drive a batter off the plate or, in some circumstances, even hit him with a pitch as long as the ball is thrown well below the neckline. Terms associated with this act include *bean* and *beanball, dust* and *duster, brush* and *brushback, knockdown, shave,* and *barber.* It is sometimes called a *purpose pitch* or *chin music.*

1.5.1. "Message" Pitches Should Always Be a "Batting-Practice Fastball" to the Middle of the Back or the Butt

This is where revenge and civility shake hands. Dave Kaplan, who works with Yogi Berra as director of the Yogi Berra Museum & Learning Center on the campus of Montclair State

University in Little Falls, New Jersey, reports: "I've heard Yogi talk in the past that he occasionally would be knocked down if he had great success against a pitcher. In particular Dizzy Trout. However, Trout would actually tell Yogi beforehand he had to throw at him, so get ready. And Trout, apparently because he respected him, would bean him in the behind, which Yogi never minded ('that was OK, it didn't hurt back there')."

1.5.2. Above-the-Neckline Pitches Can Be Used for More Serious Messages—but Are Increasingly Controversial and Are Regarded as a Life-and-Death Issue

This unwritten rule was at the heart of the altercation between thirty-one-year-old Pedro Martinez and seventy-two-year-old Don Zimmer in the Red Sox's 4–3 loss to the Yankees in Game 3 of the ALCS on October 11, 2003. Martinez violated the unwritten rule when he threw behind the head of New York's Karim Garcia. In the Red Sox half of the inning, Manny Ramirez half-charged the mound with his bat in his hand after taking a nose-high Roger Clemens fastball that was actually over the plate. A bench-clearing brawl ensued, during which Zimmer charged Martinez and ended up on the ground. Zimmer, a pre-batting-helmet victim of a beanball with a plate in his head to prove it, took on the role of enforcer of the unwritten rule. Manager Joe Torre alluded to Zimmer's 1953 beaning in a postgame interview, adding, "He was unconscious for a week when he did get hit in the head."

"Baseball might be a sylvan pastime in May. In October, it's a hard, mean game played to the limit. That's why it has rules. And the most important rules are the unwritten ones," wrote Michael Gee of the *Boston Herald* in his account of this incident, in which he claims that Martinez violated both the unwritten rule against throwing at a man's head and also one that says you don't show how tough you are with an aging baseball legend. In the process, Martinez upset the equilibrium of the Red Sox. The next morning, Tom Boswell asked in the *Washington Post*, " . . . is a septuagenarian coach eligible for the ALCS most valuable player award?"

A pitch intentionally thrown at a batter's head is known as a "beanball," and the practice itself is known as "headhunting." When such practices get out of hand, they are known as "beanball wars" and make for chilling headlines, such as back in 1987, when a July cover of *Sports Illustrated* had the headline, "Beanbrawls: Baseball's Headhunting Wars Get Ugly," and an August *Christian Science Monitor* headline read, "Baseball Must Act to Defuse Beanball Wars."

Beanballs have a long tradition in baseball, and some people actually celebrate the practice without apology. "One of the greatest and most effective balls pitched is the 'bean ball' . . . and pitching at the batter's head, not to hit it, but to drive him out of position and perhaps cause him to get panic-stricken and swing at the ball in self-defense is an art" is how it was depicted by John J. Evers and Hugh Fullerton in an article in the *St. Louis Post-Dispatch* on May 3, 1910.

The only player ever killed in a major-league game was Ray Chapman of the Cleveland Indians, who was hit in the head by a pitch thrown by Carl Mays of the New York Yankees on August 16, 1920, and died twelve hours later. But there have been deaths at other levels of the game. Bill James, the game's most notable man of numbers, counts four minor leaguers killed by beanballs between 1909 and 1920, and notes a chilling headline in the *San Francisco Call-Bulletin* on September 23, 1947: "'Bean Ball' Is Fatal to S. F. Sandlotter."

But most of the ardent lovers of baseball cannot find a justification for the practice. "I realize I'm preaching against 'time-honored tradition,'" Stew Thornley wrote in a pointed essay for the online discussion group of the Society for American Baseball Research (August 6, 2001), but the concept of drilling a batter as a means of behavior modification is barbaric. Whenever I bring this up, I can count on someone recounting tales of those tough old pitchers like Wynn and Drysdale and Gibson. However, I've never seen that as justification for the practice—then or now. . . . Seems to me if a pitcher really is that tough, he wouldn't do his dirty work 60 feet away. If Davey Lopes has a problem with Rickey Henderson, why doesn't he confront him face-to-face rather than order one of his pitchers to intentionally hit him with a pitch? As unsavory as it is, I'd even give Lopes more credit if he took a punch at Rickey. That's not a good thing, but it would at least take some guts.

Thomley adds this in extended discussion of the practice:

There is an ebb and flow to the practice of head-hunting and pitches meant to inflict bodily harm. Hugh Casey was a pitcher for the Brooklyn Dodgers and one of the most deliberate purpose pitchers in the 1940s. In 1946, Casey became the first pitcher to throw a beaner at a hitter standing outside the batter's box. After entering a game against the St. Louis Cardinals, Casey was taking his warm-up pitches when he noticed that Marty Marion, the batter due up, was standing six feet from the batter's circle, timing his deliveries and swinging his bat each time Casey's warm-up tosses crossed the plate. Casey yelled at Marion, telling him to stop it, and Marion hollered back in defiance. The next pitch from Casey sailed at Marion's head, sending the shortstop to the ground.

At the SABR convention in 1997, I heard Jim Bunning tell how he drilled Mickey Mantle because someone in the New York dugout was figuring out what pitch he was going to throw and whistling as a signal to the batter. I couldn't understand why Mantle should have to pay for Bunning's incompetence in tipping his pitchers. Please understand that I'm not advocating fistfights; I'm only saying that I find cheap shots to be even worse.

For its part, organized baseball has taken a tough stand against the practice and umpires have been instructed to be proactive in eliminating as much head-hunting as possible. Today's umpires are likely to issue warnings or eject potential offenders quicker than ever before. Major League Baseball has a "Heads Up" program in which all crews are required to report incidents or potential incidents that might lead to incidents in the future. MLB then alerts the crew handling games later in the season that an inciting incident has occurred and to be especially vigilant for any carryover. No longer is there the philosophy of letting a team "get even" before issuing a warning.

1.5.3. If Your Pitcher Hits One of Our Batters, We Will Hit One of Yours

This is known as the "law of retaliation": an unwritten understanding among players that if a pitcher on team A throws at a batter on team B, the pitcher on team B will throw at a batter on team A rather than confront the pitcher directly or charge the mound. Umpire Tom Gorman (*Three and Two!* 1979) wrote: "If an opposing pitcher knocks down one of his teammates, a player expects his pitcher to get even and knock down the other pitcher, or one of the opposition players. It's part of the baseball code."

Of course, where above-the-neck pitches are concerned, retaliation is not a trivial matter, especially when such things become a question of life and death—or, at the very least, long-term or career-ending bodily harm. The larger dilemma that the rule of retaliation creates is that intentionally hitting a batter is condoned at every level of the game through the minors and into college ball, if not further. Yet Major League Baseball rules specifically forbid pitchers from intentionally throwing at a batter. Such conduct "is unsportsmanlike and highly dangerous. It should be—and is—condemned by everybody." (See *Official Rules of Major League Baseball*, rule 8.02 (d), comment.) Violators are subject to sanctions, including ejection from the game.

But intimidation can be fashioned into a philosophy of the game, which from time to time is displayed with bravado. The late Billy Martin was a case in point. When he was a manager, "Billyball," as his baseball philosophy came to be known, combined speed, daring, and fundamentals, but at bottom it was based on Martin's willingness to intimidate—even if that meant ordering his pitchers to throw at batters.

Virtually ignored by the mainstream press, including most significantly the nation's newspaper sports pages and the slick sports magazines, was a 2006 court decision that essentially blessed the practice of intentionally throwing a baseball at a man's head despite its prohibition in the official rules of the game. The unwritten rule trumped the written rule, and the official rules were deemed to be irrelevant. An intentional beaning was relegated to an inherent risk of the game, in the same category as a hard tackle in football or a knockout punch in boxing. (There is a problem with the boxing analogy, because the object of the sport is to win, including by KO, while the object of baseball is not to bean a batter. Likewise, the object of defense in football is to tackle players. A more apt comparison would be a helmet-to-helmet hit in football rather than a hard tackle—the latter is a legal play, while the former is gratuitous and illegal.)

The legal case dealt with two community college teams playing in a 2001 preseason practice game in which a nineteen-year-old named Jose Avila, of the Rio Hondo Roadrunners, was hit in the head by a pitch from a pitcher for the Citrus Community College Owls. The pitch, which cracked his helmet, was thrown in retaliation after the Roadrunners pitcher hit an Owls batter. At the time of the original lawsuit, Avila suffered from sporadic seizures and sued the Citrus Community College District, alleging, among other things, the district was negligent for failing to control participating pitchers.

After Avila won in a lower court, the case went to the California Supreme Court, which in April 2006 ruled 6–1 that a community college baseball player could not sue to recover damages from an opposing school even though he was intentionally beaned and suffered physically because of the beaning. "Being hit by a pitch is an inherent risk of baseball," Justice Kathryn Mickle Werdegar wrote for the majority. It is "so accepted by custom that a pitch intentionally thrown at a batter has its own terminology: 'brushback,' 'beanball,' 'chin music.'" "For better or worse," Werdegar wrote, "being intentionally thrown at is a fundamental and inherent risk of the sport of baseball. It is not the function of tort law to police such conduct. Even if the Citrus College pitcher intentionally threw at Avila, his conduct did not fall outside the range of ordinary activity involved in the sport." Citing a long line of cases, the justices reversed an appeals court that ruled that the batter could sue for damages, and as precedent for their decision, cited a long list of headhunters, dating back to Sal "the Barber" Maglie, who claimed that his .657 won-lost percentage over ten major-league seasons during the 1950s would not have been possible without "the knock-down pitch, the so-called bean ball."

"The majority holds that a baseball pitcher owes no duty to refrain from intentionally throwing a baseball at an opposing player's head. This is a startling conclusion," Justice Joyce Kennard wrote as the sole dissenter, citing the official rules of Major League Baseball, which does not permit such conduct. Or at least strives to keep it under control—especially balls aimed at a batter's head. There is much more "mind reading" today on the part of umpires, who will issue a warning on a hunch that a drilling is about to take place. "There has been a progression in the checks and balances of baseball. Umpires have more power to assume that a person is likely to be headhunting," says Peter Schmuck of the *Baltimore Sun,* who has been a beat baseball writer for more than thirty years. So, too, he insists that the days when Bob Gibson ruled the plate and demanded total surrender from batters, and when Don Drysdale would rather send a batter to first base with a bruise than on a clean base hit, have given way to a time of a greater balance of terror.

Schmuck recalls being at a disciplinary hearing in New York in the mid-1980s at which American League president Dr. Bobby Brown was meting out discipline for a dangerous above-the-neck pitch and gave what seemed to Schmuck a very mild punishment. Schmuck questioned the ruling, and Brown shot back, "It's not a tea party." Schmuck adds: "I think about that all the time. Brown was a former player and a physician and understood the dynamics of the game."

1.6.0. A Pitcher Can't Overtly Apologize if He Accidentally Hits a Batter

Pitcher Todd Jones has this take on this unwritten rule: "There are ways to get your point across, try to make eye contact, but if you can't, you don't say anything there. You can call over to the clubhouse after the game. My teammates don't want to hear me say, 'HEY man, I'm sorry . . .'; they want him to think it's on purpose so he's not comfortable the next time I face him."

This can be most confusing to fans who think that a purpose pitch should be just that and not mixed in with a "not-on-purpose" pitch. As one anonymous respondent put it in a discussion of unwritten rules on a baseball blog: "If a pitcher would apologize for his accident, it could derail many potential brawls. It also makes a true knockdown pitch more effective; if the pitcher doesn't apologize, the batter will really know what the pitcher is doing."

1.7.0. Basebrawls Are a Rare but Necessary Part of the Game, with Their Own Set of Rules

There are times when the action of your opponent is so far over the line that the only answer is to duke it out on the field in a battle royale in which no one is actually likely to get hurt. It is a ritual closer to ballet than a true street fight.

1.7.1. In a Fight, Everyone Must Leave the Bench and the Bullpen Has to Join In

"No teammates are closer than they are in baseball, because there are so many games and players spend so much time with one another," writes ESPN's Tim Kurkjian. "As corny as it sounds, they become family, and when a family member is in a fight, everyone joins in. If a player doesn't run on the field, even if it's just to dance with the enemy, he might get fined and certainly will be ostracized by his teammates." Teams become something of a family over the course of a long season, developing an "all-for-one" mentality, and everyone goes out there to push and shove.

There is a practical purpose to everybody going on the field, which is that it actually reduces the chance of anyone actually getting hurt. Writer Patrick Hruby has called "Base-brawl Etiquette" a code of conduct "as rigidly mannered as one of the dutiful, repressed English butlers in a Merchant-Ivory film." One of the reasons that everyone is so willing to get into the faux battle is that everyone knows that when the dust settles, nothing much will really have happened, and it is rare that anyone will have been hurt.

The extent to which this rule is observed can lapse into the extreme. During a 1984 Atlanta Braves–San Diego Padres scuffle, injured Brave Bob Horner—who was watching the game from the press box—raced down to the clubhouse, put on his uniform, and ended up in the middle of the brawl. Indians manager Charlie Manuel was once suspended for two games for running onto the field from the clubhouse. Manuel had been ejected from the game, but said he could not in good conscience stay in the clubhouse while his players were throwing haymakers.

1.7.2. All Basebrawls Are Clean:
No Cleats, No Sucker Punches, and No Bats

Baseball fights normally are tame endeavors that do not last more than a few minutes, but every now and then, they get ugly and become donnybrooks. Former Brewers center fielder Gorman Thomas recalled a fight with New York during which Yankees pitcher Luis Tiant emerged from the tunnel and into the dugout wrapped only in a towel and smoking a cigar. "It wasn't a pretty sight," said Thomas to Tom Haudricourt of the *Milwaukee Journal Sentinel*. But even here there were no cheap shots from behind. "If you are going to fight, do it face-to-face" is the prime rule in play. This is not to say that baseball fights cannot become violent affairs. There are many examples of these, but none so graphic as Juan Marichal's use of a bat against John Roseboro on August 22, 1965. Fourteen stitches were required to close the gash in Roseboro's head.

1.7.3. When in Doubt, Dogpile

A dogpile is a tussle that begins between two opposing players who are quickly buried under a human avalanche. Why dogpile? It protects the combatants and keeps the whole thing from getting out of control. There is a saying in baseball that the safest place to be in a fight is in the middle of it—or in this case, the bottom of it.

1.7.4. Batters Should Never Charge the Mound for a Ball Thrown below the Neck

"I was hit 198 times," Hall of Famer Frank Robinson told *Sporting News* in a 1993 interview. "I never went to the mound once. When I played, it was just part of the game. That was one of the things that pitchers had a right to do. It was a common thing, an unwritten rule. It was accepted."

1.8.0. Do Not Fraternize with Members of the Opposition during the Regular Season

This rule does not apply in spring training and goes out of play at the end of the season. It also does not apply when players are out of uniform.

1.8.1. Players Can Talk to Each Other—but Not Face-to-Face

For instance, a man reaching first on a walk might chat with the first baseman about his golf game, but only while both are looking toward home plate.

1.8.2. Catchers Are Allowed to Talk to Batters, but Never after the Pitch Has Begun

Dave Kaplan, who works with Yogi Berra as director of the Yogi Berra Museum & Learning Center on the campus of Montclair State University in Little Falls, New Jersey, reports that Yogi was always accused of distracting hitters with chit-chat behind the plate. But he adamantly denies ever talking to hitters during a pitch. He was just trying to be sociable. And if a guy didn't want to talk to him, he wouldn't talk back. He always had a great running dialogue with Ted Williams, and both were very friendly. Yogi would ask him where he was going fishing, if he had been to any good movies, and so on. And Ted loved chatting with Yogi. However, Yogi remembered there was one time Williams was in a pretty foul mood, and finally turned to Yogi and said, "OK, I'm here to hit. Shut up, you little Dago." But the next day they resumed their chatting with each other.

1.9.0. There Is No Crying in Baseball

One of the tenets of baseball stoicism is for players to show no soft emotions during competition.

One of the most recalled of all scenes in any baseball movie is this interchange from *A League of Their Own* (1992), in which the Tom Hanks character, manager Jimmy Dugan, schools Evelyn Gardner, who is played by Bitty Schram.

It begins as Dugan chews out a player, Evelyn Gardner, for throwing home with a two-run lead, allowing the tying run to take second. He tells her to start using her head—"That's the lump that's three feet above your ass."

With this Evelyn begins to cry, and Dugan responds: "Are you crying? Are you crying? ARE YOU CRYING? There's no crying! THERE'S NO CRYING IN BASEBALL!"

Doris Murphy chimes in to ask him to give Evelyn a break.

He answers: "Oh, you zip it, Doris! Rogers Hornsby was my manager, and he called me a talking pile of pigshit. And that was when my parents drove all the way down from Michigan to see me play the game. And did I cry?" He asks Evelyn to tell him why he didn't cry, but she can't, so he hammers the point home: "THERE'S NO CRYING IN BASEBALL! No crying!"

1.9.1. Hugging is Tolerated in Baseball, but Only Recently

Such is the nature of the game that baseball celebrates the fact that Tommy Lasorda was the first manager to have hugged one of his players. When Joe Torre accepted the job as new manager of the Los Angeles Dodgers, he admitted he didn't think much of it when Lasorda began the practice of hugging players. "Now look where we are," Torre said on that occasion, grinning. "We hug at the drop of a hat." As if to prove the point, new manager Torre and Tommy Lasorda hugged for the cameras during the team's first official day of workouts at the Dodgertown training complex in Vero Beach, Florida, on February 15, 2008. Now there are players that hug.

1.10.0. Never Show Pain Inflicted by an Opponent, No Matter How Much It Hurts

1.11.0. There Is No Rubbing in Baseball

1.11.1. When Hit by the Ball, Never Rub It—Even When It Is Not on Purpose

1.11.2. Never Rub Yourself after a Collision, Including Hard Slides and Head-on Collisions at Home Plate

At every level of the game, this is seen as a sign of weakness and vulnerability—even if the hit is accidental.

Joe Garagiola again, this time about asserting himself on his first swing around the National League, speaking about a generalized opponent facing him as a catcher: "He's going to bowl you over to score that run. Brace yourself, and don't rub when you get up. It's you or him. You can't call for help, and you can't go home."

1.12.0. Baseball Has Unwritten Small Rituals That Often Defy Logic

1.12.1. As a Pitcher, Always Walk Off the Field at the End of an Inning; for All Other Players, the Rule Is Run On, Run Off the Field

1.12.2. After the Last Out in an Inning That Has Been Made by an Outfielder, Always Toss the Ball to the Fans, but Never Ever Pretend That You Will Toss It to a Fan and Then Not Do So

1.12.3. At the End of Practice, When the Coach Asks, "Are There Any Questions?" Never Respond

1.13.0. Respect the Other Team—Do Not "Show Up" the Opposition

Essentially, the accepted baseball code dictates that players do whatever they can to win without embarrassing opponents or overvaluing individual achievements. Tim Keown has discussed (in *ESPN the Magazine,* June 25, 2001) the baseball code at length. He noted that the code's most stringent statutes deal with blowouts, "when the losing team is most susceptible to frustration, anger and embarrassment": don't swing at a 3–0 pitch, steal after the sixth inning, stretch singles into doubles, or exhibit excessive pride in your own accomplishments in a game you lead by five or more runs.

Buck Martinez, as manager of Blue Jays, said: "If you hit a home run and strut around the bases, you make a fool of yourself and the game. When you cross that line, anything goes. I think the biggest violation of the unwritten rules is that someone disrespects the game. . . . It's a great game and nobody should disrespect the game nor should he express anger towards the pitcher when popping up or striking out. Pitchers should not strike a man out and celebrate with a display of celebratory gyrations."

1.13.1. Especially after a Home Run Is Hit

A batter should not show up the pitcher by taking time to admire a home run as it sails over the wall or display any other histrionic excess such as flipping the bat in the air or taking a long time circling the bases in a one-man tribute to himself. As Larry Stone of the *Seattle Times* put it: "The home run is the hard work. It's what happens afterward that separates the boys of summer from the showmen." Historically, this was inviolable. Chicago Cubs manager Phil Cavarretta once said of Ernie Banks, the only man to earn the honorific of "Mr. Baseball," "After he hits a homer, he comes back to the bench looking like he did something wrong." George F. Will has written that Mickey Mantle ran the bases with his head down, "almost as if he worries that he has done something ostentatious."

And there was a time when pitchers like Sal Maglie and Bob Gibson and Don Drysdale did not let anyone celebrate hitting one of their pitches out of the park, because the next pitch would be thrown to punish.

Because almost all games are now televised and because cable television maintains a 24/7 eye on the game that feeds on highlights, there is a lot of pressure on this rule, and it is sometimes abused. John Feinstein wrote in the *Washington Post* that anyone playing one of the major sports "knows that the way to make the highlight shows isn't to hit a jump shot or a home run, it is to dunk and dance; score a touchdown and salute; or hit a home run and pose." The result in baseball is the proliferation of such antics. "I think there is too much on both sides. Pitchers showing up batters and batters showing up pitchers," said Tony La Russa when asked about excesses after a home run.

But showing up the other guy still brings strong disapproval and in most quarters is still a serious transgression. Said Sam Perlozzo when he was the Baltimore Orioles' skipper: "If there is one basic unwritten rule for me it is not to try and show the other guy up."

"Don't show up your opponent. Just play the game and don't get too outrageous," said Leon Roberts, Cincinnati Reds hitting coordinator. "Hit a home run, run around the bases, head down, halfway fast instead of dancing around, prancing around. That's how you end up getting drilled." There was a time when punishment might not come until the next season in spring training. In 1987, Boston pitcher Al Nipper drilled Darryl Strawberry in retribution for Strawberry's flamboyant trot on a home run in Game 7 of the 1986 World Series.

Three names from the recent baseball past—Baltimore Oriole Cal Ripken Jr., San Diego Padre Tony Gwynn, and New York Yankee Paul O'Neill (players seen as the "soul" of their franchises for a good number of years)—are mentioned time and again in interviews on this subject as "poster boys" for observing this unofficial rule. "A guy like Paul O'Neill was the ultimate pro," said Jeff Torborg the year after O'Neill hung up his spikes. "He didn't even look up on the ones he hit because he didn't want to show anybody up." Don Mattingly, former spring-training instructor of the New York Yankees, said in 2002: "If I hit a home run I would just run the bases. Not throw the bat or anything." Mattingly cuts a little slack for those who are a bit more "emotional," but he adds, "But you still have to show respect for the game." Reflecting on the unwritten rule against showing up the opposition, Joe Torre uses a football analogy: "When I brag about my club, I say we don't spike the ball." (Torre is fascinated by the rituals of football as they contrast to baseball. "A guy does this dance after running 40 yards and his team is still down by 40 points. Amazing.")

Violators of this rule are recalled long after their playing career is over. The aforementioned San Francisco Giant Jeffrey Leonard, for instance, was still being cited in 2008 as an example of a transgressor for his 1987 practice of rounding the bases with one arm tucked in to his side, which he called his "one flap down" trot. Now, as then, it is described with the term *chickensh***.

Ditto for Sammy Sosa with his full array of heart tugs and skyward gestures, which amused for a while but which have, over time, become as tiresome as the Macarena. And perhaps one of the reasons Barry Bonds will be recalled with disdain by future generations is because of the way he posed after he hit a home run. The late David Halberstam called him "The Great Narcissist," and wrote of his home-run machinations: "The pause at this moment, as we have all come to learn, is very long, plenty of time for the invisible but Zen-like moment of appreciation when Barry Bonds psychically high-fives Barry Bonds and reassures him once again that there's no one quite like him in baseball."

Larry Bowa admits that "style points," which were forbidden in the past, are becoming more and more accepted in the twenty-first century. "A guy like Schmidty, he would just put his head down and go around the bases especially with a pitcher like Bob Gibson or Nolan Ryan on the mound," he said, referring to Hall of Fame third baseman Mike Schmidt.

One thing that is clear is that the fear of being shown up keeps showboating in check. "Does the batter who postures after a home run want that same pitcher to posture when he strikes him out on his next at bat?" asks John Mizerock, bullpen coach of the Kansas City Royals.

Paul White of *USA Today Sports Weekly* said that he once asked Ken Griffey Jr. about his most memorable home run. "He had two. The first was when he went back to back with his dad. The other was the first ball he ever hit over a fence in Little League. He said: 'I went around the bases like Steve

Garvey in the playoffs, and when I got back to the dugout my dad was waiting for me. I have never ever, ever done anything like that again. I'm even reluctant to pump my fist when I hit a walkoff to win a game.'"

1.13.2. Do Not Steal a Base or Bunt
When Your Team Has a Big Lead Late in a Game

Taking an extra base or bunting when your team has a safe lead in the final innings is considered kicking an opposing team when it's down. "Don't ever manage to embarrass your opponent," said Seattle skipper Lou Piniella to a *Seattle Times* reporter in 2001. A few days earlier, the Mariners led Kansas City by eight runs in the eighth, and the swift Charles Gipson was held up at third while running from second when a single was hit to right field. Piniella had simply shut down the running game in deference to a team he would face again.

But what is a safe lead? The answer to this question gives this rule considerable flexibility. Braves manager Bobby Cox has said that one rule of thumb that managers have used is not to let a grand slam beat them. In other words, if they have a five-run lead late in the game, that should be sufficient.

Stealing a base with a five-run lead was over the line in earlier eras, but not today to a manager who has to play in Boston or Denver, where a five-run lead is by no means safe. It can also depend on the other variables. Recalling his days managing in Chicago, former Yankees bench coach Don Zimmer said: "If you have a big lead in Wrigley with the wind blowing in, you are pretty safe with a five-run lead. But if the wind is blowing out, an eight-run lead could be gone in two innings, so you really don't know." A real-world example of how difficult this is to solve: Seattle manager Lou Piniella and Cleveland skipper Charlie Manuel removed key players during what appeared to be a Seattle rout on August 5, 2001—the Mariners led 14–2—only to watch as the Indians came from behind to win in the eleventh by a final score of 15–14.

There are those who have openly violated this rule. The late Syd Thrift, a former Baltimore Orioles vice president of baseball operations who came up in the Yankees organization, told me: "I can remember Casey Stengel saying at one time when he had a lead of nine or ten runs, he still stole bases. If people got mad with him, Stengel said, 'If you can guarantee me that you won't score more runs than this, I'll stop running.'"

A case in point took place in July 2001, when Ricky Henderson took second base in the seventh inning of a game in which his San Diego Padres led Davey Lopes's Milwaukee

Brewers 12–5. Lopes went ballistic because he felt Henderson had violated the unwritten rule. Lopes was so infuriated that he stopped the game, strolled to second base, and publicly chastised Henderson, threatening to drill him in his next at bat. Henderson was removed from the game, preventing retaliation, but Lopes followed that display with strong words in a postgame interview. "There are unwritten rules in baseball," he said. "They were there before I was born, there while I'm here and they'll be there after I'm long gone. That's not going to change."

All of this drew the attention of Frank Robinson, then lord of discipline for Major League Baseball. Robinson levied a two-game suspension and an undisclosed fine, and Lopes took his punishment without appealing the decision. Later, Lopes admitted that he should have handled the situation differently; that is, a bit more discreetly. But he didn't back down from his contention that one of baseball's "unwritten rules" was breached. "As far as what I feel is necessary to stop people from exploiting this game at certain times, I don't think anybody would tolerate it," said Lopes.

Although criticized for his threats, Lopes had his defenders. "I think it's a shame that there are some teams that will not shut down with a five-run lead in a late inning," said Mike Hargrove, Baltimore Orioles manager at the time of the incident. One of those would be Charlie Manuel, then manager of the Cleveland Indians: "If I can beat you 20–0, I'm going to beat you 20–0."

"It's always been a dicey issue," said Tim McCarver, a veteran of 1,909 career games, to Kevin Kelly of the *St. Petersburg Times* when asked about not running up the score. "But for the most part, for the guys who've played the game, it's right, it's respectful and it's the way the game should be played." In 1967, Reds pitcher Don Nottebart believed the Cardinals's Lou Brock was wrong for trying to steal during a game believed out of reach and later beaned Brock to incite a brawl. "It was a huge fight," McCarver told Kelly. "A policeman ended up having his jaw broken."

Despite this, there always seems to be examples of this rule being broken. In 2003, when the Red Sox beat the Florida Marlins, 25–8, at Fenway, losing manager Jack McKeon said to anyone who would listen, "I didn't realize your pitching was that bad over here that you would try to add on to a 16-run lead in the seventh inning." On a play at the plate to end the seventh inning, the Red Sox tried to turn a fly ball to shallow center field into a sacrifice fly with the score 21–5. Then there was the August 22, 2007, Rangers-Orioles 30–3 rout when Texas scored most of its runs in the final three innings, allowing one of their relievers to earn a save while pitching with a twenty-seven-run lead. The Rangers became the first team in 110 years to score thirty runs in a game. "The Rangers manager, it seems, is guilty of allowing his team to pour it on when restraint was in order," wrote one fan on the official Orioles Magic Web site. "There's a reason why these games are so rare—most managers know when to tell their players to quit. An unwritten code, to prevent complete humiliation. When you break the code, there can be consequences."

In a letter published in the January/February 2006 issue of *Baseball Digest,* a reader claimed that a lead is never safe and then listed a half dozen games—three from each league—in which teams overcame twelve-run deficits. The earliest of these games was played on June 18, 1911, when the Tigers trailed the White Sox at Detroit, 13–1, going into the bottom of the fourth inning, but won 16–15.

Zack Hample, author of *Watching Baseball Smarter,* argues that from the standpoint of the paying customer, this unwritten rule is, to use his word, "crap." He said, "Fans should get a refund if one of the teams essentially stops trying to score." One of the reasons the rule is being ignored more often today is that incentive clauses in player contracts do not distinguish between walk-off homers and homers hit when your team is up by ten runs.

1.13.3. In a Blowout Game, Never
Swing as Hard as You Can at a 3–0 Pitch

"I remember when B. J. Surhoff was a rookie, he took this big swing against Nolan Ryan," former Brewers second baseman Jim Gantner said in an interview with the *Milwaukee Journal Sentinel.* "Everybody on the bench said, 'Watch this next pitch.' Nolan gave him that high, inside heat. B.J. went flying back. Everybody in the dugout was laughing."

1.13.4. Do Not Steal Signs
Late in the Game in a Blowout

1.13.5. Do Not Bring In Your Closer
When He Is Not Needed

The exception here is that when a team has had a string of games that do not involve save situations, the manager might bring in a closer in a lopsided game just to give him an inning of work and keep him sharp.

1.13.6. Do Not Try to Pick Off a Base Runner When Your Team Has a Big Lead

1.13.7. Do Not Clear Your Bench or Try Guys at Different Positions during a Blowout

1.14.0. Always Use a Good, Clean, Hard Slide to Break Up a Double Play

Middle infielders are at their most vulnerable when turning a double play, so any slide perceived as "dirty" or intended to injure is taboo. Roll blocks have been outlawed because of the number of infielders injured over the years. Former Milwaukee Brewers second baseman Jim Gantner blew out a knee one year when New York's Marcus Lawton roll blocked him, leading to a melee between the clubs. "You go in hard and clean to try to break up two," Gantner told Tom Haudricourt of the *Milwaukee Journal Sentinel* in August 2001. "I don't think [Lawton] did it intentionally, but you can't go in like that."

1.15.0 Never, Ever Slide into the Infielder with Your Spikes High

This is not to say that there is not an occasional player who flirts with the thoughts articulated by Ty Cobb when he said that the base paths belonged to him. The rules gave him the right, and if the baseman was standing in the way and got hurt by Cobb's spikes, it was the baseman's fault.

1.16.0. Run Hard to First on a Ground Ball

As simple as this seems, it is still an issue that surfaces from time to time and one of the situations in which a player is expected to apologize to his teammates. Boston's Manny Ramirez made this blunder in the third inning of a September 9, 2002, game against the Tampa Bay Devil Rays, embarrassing himself and his teammates. According to Michael Silverman in the *Boston Herald:* "He redeemed himself, at least partially, by immediately apologizing to his teammates once he got back to the dugout. Two plate appearances later, Ramirez made further amends by hitting the go-ahead home run in the Red Sox' eventual 6–3 victory."

1.17.0. There Are No-hitter Protocols in Baseball—Not Always Observed but Always Noted with Passion

1.17.1. Don't Mention a No-hitter or Perfect Game in Progress

"One of the oldest baseball superstitions is the unwritten rule that specifies no one is ever to mention that a no-hitter is being manufactured," wrote Arthur Daley of the *New York Times* back in 1959, adding: "Only a scoundrel would commit so dastardly a deed, because such mention instantly brings the whammy out of hiding. The whammy is a spook with the horns of a jinx that would thereupon direct the flight of the next batted ball and destroy the no-hitter."

1.17.1.1. A Pitcher Closing In on a No-hitter Should Not Acknowledge the Fact by Talking or Even Thinking about It

Dating back to a time before radio or television broadcasters became part of this taboo, it is believed that when a pitcher hears the word "no-hitter," the spell accounting for this hard-to-achieve feat will be broken and the no-hitter lost. The concept was that the knowledge would be a distraction to a man whose thoughts were supposed to be concentrated on the batter at hand. This even extends to the man pitching the no-hitter. But violators in the person of the pitchers themselves began to occasionally flaunt the unwritten rule during the era when Daley was writing his column for the *Times* (1942–1973). "Think I can get the no-hitter?" Yankees pitcher Allie Reynolds asked Eddie Lopat as they sat on the bench during the seventh inning of a 1951 no-hitter. Lopat was horrified and reminded him of the rule. "I can read," Reynolds shot back, "It's right there on the scoreboard." Then there was the July 1958 game in which the Tigers' Jim Bunning defied the rule to the point where it was reported as the "gabbiest no-hitter on record" by mentioning it on a number of occasions in the later innings of the game. "Protect the no-hitter boys," he bellowed to his teammates as they took the field for the eighth inning. "Start diving for everything. It's getting close."

1.17.1.2. Teammates Should Never Mention the Feat to the Pitcher at the Point They Realize What Is at Stake

On October 8, 1956, when the New York Yankees' Don Larsen pitched his perfect game in the World Series, the only no-hitter in Series history, this rule was perfectly observed. It was one of the greatest moments in baseball history, and one that Larsen recalled in a 1996 *Sports Illustrated* interview. After Larsen had set down the Dodgers in the seventh, he realized what might happen. Sitting in the dugout, a lit cigarette in his hand, he stared out at the scoreboard and saw the string of zeros. "Hey, Mick," said Larsen to Mickey Mantle, who was beside him. "Look at that. Two more innings. Wouldn't it be something."

Mantle stood up and walked away without saying a word. At that point, superstition ruled the Yankees' dugout. No one dared mention the no-hitter or even talk to Larsen. The dugout, usually full of banter, fell suddenly silent. "It was lonely in there those last two innings," Larsen recalled. "The only time I felt comfortable was when I was on the mound."

Joe Torre, who had witnessed the Larsen game from the upper deck of Yankee Stadium as a sixteen-year-old, was in the dugout as the Yankees' manager on May 17, 1998, when he realized in the fourth inning of a game against the Minnesota Twins that David Wells was in a position to throw a no-hitter. After Wells struck out the first two Minnesota hitters in the sixth, and the inning ended with an easy fly out, everyone in the stadium had noticed it: Wells had a no-hitter going. He walked into a wall of cheers as he left the mound in the sixth. But his teammates seemed to deliberately avoid him, and the dugout again became silent. Wells wanted to speak to Jorge Posada, his catcher, but Posada fled to the other end of the dugout. Wells then sat down next to Darryl Strawberry, who promptly got up and walked away. "They were killing me, man," Wells said after the game. He went on to pitch the fifteenth perfect game in history. Comedian and Yankees fan extraordinaire Billy Crystal walked into the clubhouse after the game, approached David Wells, and said, "I got here late, what happened?"

The parallels between the two perfect games extended beyond the behavior in the dugout. "I think it's something that won't ever happen again," Larsen told *Sports Illustrated* in December 1998, after the Wells feat. "Two guys from the same high school [Point Loma High, in San Diego] throwing perfect games. We'll always be linked, and that's fine with me. I can relate to him, especially the fun-loving part, doing things you like to do in life outside of baseball. I've done some crazy things, too. Life's no fun unless you get out and enjoy it."

(In the wake of the Wells perfect game was an ad in the long-running ESPN "This is SportsCenter" campaign. "Every once in a while" [says anchor Stuart Scott] "it all just comes together and you have a perfect show: Bob Ley in '89; Charley Steiner had his in '91; Dan [Patrick] had one working last season ... During the commercial breaks, the crew wouldn't talk to him. [Coanchor] Kenny [Mayne] wouldn't even look at him. Only one segment left. Can Dan do it?" [Says Patrick:] "That, of course, is the sort of thing that can't never happen in a play-off race." [Voice-over:] "A double negative. No perfect show.")

1.17.1.3. Broadcasters Should Not Utter Either of the Terms No-hitter or Perfect Game before the Feat Is Accomplished, Lest It Jinx the Proceedings

This taboo is also observed by many sports broadcasters, who use various linguistic subterfuges to inform their listeners that the pitcher has not given up a hit, never saying "no-hitter." Probably the most famous example of a baseball broadcaster taking this into another realm was President Ronald Reagan, who deferred questions about upcoming elections by citing this taboo, which operated during his days broadcasting Chicago Cubs games. Asked in 1984 if he thought the presidential election would be close, he said that he never mentioned no-hitters on broadcasts as they unfolded. "I kind of feel the same way about campaigning," he said.

But there are those who insist on blabbing without a moment of hesitation. As Felix Hernandez advanced toward a possible no-hitter against the Red Sox on April 11, 2007, Mariners broadcaster Dave Sims told his viewers about it, superstitions be damned. "I was all over it," Sims told the *Seattle Times*. "I'm looking at the line score while we were going to breaks, and it said no hits, so you talk about it. I'm a reporter, too." Sims's decision irked a few viewers—some of whom e-mailed the *Seattle Times* to complain. They thought Sims should have adhered to the baseball tradition of not mentioning a no-no. "It's one thing in the clubhouse or the dugout that they don't want to talk about it," Sims said. "Great. But my job, I have to tell the audience what's going on. If a guy's getting pounded, I say it. So if a guy's throwing a no-no, I have to report it." Sims was in his first year doing the Mariners' play-by-play. His radio counterpart, Dave Niehaus, has always maintained the same philosophy regarding no-hitters. On that Wednesday in Boston, when Hernandez lost his no-hitter to the first Boston hitter in the eighth, J. D. Drew, Niehaus was calling the action on KOMO radio.

"I have to be a reporter," echoed Niehaus, who estimates he has called "thirteen or fourteen" no-hitters in his long career. "From, say, the fifth inning on, certainly the sixth inning on, I've got to keep reminding people they might be sitting in on a piece of history. I'll take the wrath of people calling up. And believe me, there will be some wrath." The rule seems to be totally ignored now by ESPN and other sports networks, who will break into other coverage to show at bats of a no-hitter in progress.

Then there is the case of the New York Mets, whose pitchers had not thrown a single no-hitter through the middle of the 2008 season—a span of forty-six seasons. As Mark McGuire of the *Albany Times Union* wrote in 2007: "Major League Baseball has seen 234 no-hitters, including two this season. Five have involved the Mets. None have been thrown by one. For their uneven history, through the laughably bad 1960s leading up to the Miracle of '69, through the dark, dreary days of the late 1970s and the mediocrity of much of the 1990s, the Mets have been blessed with stellar pitching. Hall of Famers like Tom Seaver and Warren Spahn. All-stars like Dwight Gooden and Bret Saberhagen and David Cone. All those guys have no-hitters. Just not for the Mets." The closest came in 1969, when Chicago Cub Jimmy Qualls became a trivia answer by breaking up Seaver's perfect game with a one-out single in the ninth. The Mets have nineteen one-hitters to date.

McGuire then suggested: "Maybe it's the fault of the late longtime Mets' broadcaster Lindsey Nelson, who did not subscribe [to] the unwritten rule that you don't say 'no-hitter' while one [is] in progress, lest you jinx it. 'I figure, if anything I say in the broadcasting booth can influence anything going on down on the field, I ought to be getting more money,' he once said." Eight ex-Mets have thrown no-hitters, from Mike Scott to Cone. Meanwhile, nine future Mets pitched no-hitters before coming to Shea. Hideo Nomo—4–5 for New York in 1998—is the biggest insult: he threw no-hitters before and after playing in Queens.

1.17.2. Don't Bunt to Break Up a No-hitter or Perfect Game

This is an easier rule to observe when the score is out of reach. In May 2001, San Diego Padres catcher Ben Davis broke up a Curt Schilling perfect game with a bunt in the eighth inning when the Arizona Diamondbacks were leading 2–0. The Diamondbacks held on for the 2–0 victory, and Schilling finished with a three-hitter. But the bunt drew the ire of Arizona manager Bob Brenly and many others, who claimed that Davis violated the unwritten rule. Commentator Peter Gammons went as far as to say the catcher's career may "forever be marred by a bunt."

But was this a clear violation? There is a vocal minority that says that Davis was simply doing his job keeping his team in the game. "By bunting, Davis got the potential tying run to the plate. If you are still in the game there is nothing wrong with it," said Tommy Sandt, first-base coach for the Pittsburgh Pirates. Larry Stone of the *Seattle Times* may have been the most vocal: "The Diamondbacks' moral outrage over Ben Davis' bunt to break up Curt Schilling's perfect game is misguided. Essentially they are saying that baseball's arcane code of honor is more important than winning a game that might determine a playoff berth."

Historically, some of the best in the business have paid little heed to the "unwritten rules" that supposedly come into play in the late innings of no-hit and perfect games. Research conducted by indefatigable baseball scholar Al Kermisch found two examples in which stellar baseball men and future Hall of Famers had no truck with "unwritten rules." In the second game of a doubleheader in Washington on September 19, 1925, Ted Lyons of the White Sox held the Senators hitless for 8⅔ innings. Despite the fact that the White Sox held a commanding 17–0 advantage, Washington manager Bucky Harris sent veteran Bobby Veach up to pinch-hit. Veach asked the manager what he wanted him to do. "You're going up there to hit, aren't you?" replied Harris. Veach stepped to the plate and hit a sharp single to right field, breaking up the no-hitter.

Now move forward to August 5, 1932, when the great right-handed pitcher Walter Johnson was managing the AL Washington Senators, and was being beaten, 13–0, by Detroit Tiger Tommy Bridges, who needed one more out for a perfect game. Johnson took a leaf out of his old manager's book and sent Sheriff Harris, a very good pinch hitter, up to hit for pitcher Bobby Burke. The crowd of seven thousand booed lustily. The Sheriff blooped Bridges's first pitch over second base for a single. Sam Rice, the next batter, grounded out to first baseman Harry Davis, and Bridges had to be content with a one-hit shutout.

According to Kermisch, Johnson later said that he was sorry that Bridges lost his perfect game, but for himself he would not want to be credited with a perfect game if he did not earn it. Sheriff Harris's response: "I'm getting paid to hit and he's getting paid to pitch. He never gave me any breaks at the plate. Why should I give him any?"

1.18.0. The Art of Stealing Signs and Signals Has Its Own Set of Unwritten Rules

Over the course of a nine-inning baseball game, hundreds of silent signs and signals will be given and received—a thousand or more is a common estimate. Many will be false signals meant to mislead—decoys—while others will carry routine instructions, and a few may spell out the difference between winning and losing. Baseball's history is rich with gimmicky, sign-stealing schemes, but today it is a pure art based on the ability to read tip-offs and the ingenious decoding of an opponent's signs as they are being transmitted. The art of giving, receiving, and protecting signs is crucial to the game of baseball. Signs and signals are the central nervous system that allows a ball club to function as a team both offensively and defensively.

1.18.1. There Are Acceptable Forms of Sign Stealing

1.18.1.1. It Is Understood by All That Third-Base Coaches, Bench Coaches, and Others in Uniform Are Always Trying to Gain an Edge by Stealing Signals

It is assumed by anyone in uniform that at least one person on the opposing team is looking for patterns that can be decoded to the team's advantage.

1.18.1.2. A Runner on Second Who Picks Up a Signal from the Catcher Is Essentially Doing His Job, but Under the Terms of the Same Unwritten Rule

The assumption here is that if the catcher is too slow to encode his signals with a man on second, it is essentially his own fault.

1.18.1.3. However, If Any of These Forms of Acceptable Sign Stealing Becomes Obvious, Then It Becomes Unacceptable

1.18.2. There Are Unacceptable Forms of Sign Stealing

1.18.2.1. Base Runners at Second Base Shouldn't Steal a Catcher's Signs and Relay Them to the Hitter at the Plate in a Manner That Is Obvious to the Catcher

If the catcher notices the sign stealing and it is not done subtly, it is seen as a way of showing up the battery, and the batter may, as the venerable cliché goes, get a visit from Mr. Inside Fastball. In 2002, ESPN analyst and former major leaguer Harold Reynolds gave Buck Showalter an on-air tutorial on how this is done without being obvious. Reynolds said that he would be on second base, studying the opponent's catcher. He would casually put his hand on top of his head to alert the batter that he had figured out the signs. If he started his leadoff by walking off the base with his right foot, that meant that a fastball was coming. Leading with the left foot meant that a curveball had been ordered. Shuffling his feet meant that he wasn't sure what was coming. He would let his right arm dangle away from his body if the pitcher was throwing to the right side of the plate, and his left hand for the left side.

1.18.2.2. It Is Unacceptable to Steal Signs from a Point Outside the Playing Field and Dugout

1.18.2.3. It Is Unacceptable for Sign Stealers to Be Out of Uniform and/or to Employ Mechanical or Electronic Devices

The question of the ethics of sign stealing has recently been resurrected in a *Wall Street Journal* article by Joshua Harris Prager in early 2001 and expanded in his 2006 book *The Echoing Green: The Untold Story of Bobby Thomson, Ralph Branca and the Shot Heard Round the World*. Prager reexamines charges (that first surfaced in 1962) that sign stealing by means of a center-field clubhouse telescope aided the 1951 New York Giants in their improbable comeback in the weeks leading up to Bobby Thomson's famous pennant-winning home run. Prager claims the telescope was instrumental in allowing the Giants to overcome the 13½ game deficit and be in a position to win baseball's most famous pennant race.

"That's cheatin'," said Don Zimmer in the wake of the story. "If you're getting signs from a scoreboard, bullpen, using glasses, to me that's cheatin'." Virtually everyone in organized baseball agreed with Zimmer but then recalled a story in which an outsider, often using a telescope or other device, had stolen signs from a point outside the ballpark.

1.18.2.4. Peeking Back at a Catcher's Signs from the Batter's Box Is a Punishable Offense

Never peek back at the catcher to see the signs or his position while in the batter's box.

A batter in the batter's box should never turn his head back to attempt to see the catcher's signs and/or where he is positioning himself or holding his mitt as a target. The tactic of peeking is not against any written rule, but among unwritten rules, it ranks among the highest.

The great Ozzie Smith once said, "It is more important to know the location of the pitch than the type of pitch." A batter caught peeking at catchers to see where the catcher is setting up or trying to pick up signs from the plate is over the line. "In baseball, nothing is considered more verboten, or dangerous to your health, than being a sneaky peeker," writes the *Washington Post*'s Tom Boswell. "The tactic is not against any written rule, but among unwritten codes, it may rank number one."

When asking those in the game if peeking is a violation of an unwritten rule, the answers are terse and unequivocal. "That's cheating," states St. Louis Cardinals manager Tony La Russa. Broadcaster and former major-league catcher Bob Uecker has called peeking "a real no-no. Not a good idea." "If you're caught doing this," warned Dave Clark, Triple-A manager and former hitting coach for the Pittsburgh Pirates, "you're going to get hurt."

"There were some guys that did it. I never did it," said Hall of Fame third baseman George Brett. "If the catcher sets up outside, that doesn't mean that the pitch is going to be out there. So if you think that a guy is going to throw you outside and it's a fastball inside, you're dead. I was better off just seeing the ball and reacting to it."

When a peeker is spotted, retaliation can be as simple and direct as the catcher setting up outside but calling for an inside pitch. When the batter leans out toward where he thinks the pitch is going, he gets clobbered. The same fate may await those who peek at signals. In 1991, White Sox executive Ed Farmer told *Sport's Illustrated*'s Peter Gammons how Kansas City outfielder Al Cowens got his jaw broken in three places in 1979: "He peeked and saw the sign for a breaking ball away—only it was a fastball up and in." Gammons added, "It also just so happens that Farmer was the man who threw that fastball."

"Jody Davis and Bill Madlock used to peek, but the worst by far was Steve Garvey," Gary Carter, the Hall of Fame catcher who played for four teams between 1974 and 1992, said. "I'd let them know that if they kept looking, they were going down."

Do teams look for peekers? Absolutely. "In this era of field-level cameras, it's doubly dangerous to fudge." Tom Boswell said. "Teams watch those tapes. If you're a hitter, whatever you do, don't ever get caught cutting your eyes back at the catcher at the last split second to see where he's holding his mitt as a target." "There are guys who have that reputation now . . . you'd be surprised," said Texas Rangers broadcaster Tom Grieve, whose nine major-league seasons as a player in the 1970s were spent mostly with Texas. Grieve, in a 2004 *Boston Globe* interview, refused to name names. "Can't do it," Grieve added. "That's an unwritten rule with me."

This is not to say that there are not peekers who get away with it and finally come clean at the end of their careers. In *Pure Baseball*, Keith Hernandez addressed the possibility of Cecil Fielder peeking and then wrote: "Some hitters have this reputation of peeking, sometimes it's merited, sometimes it's probably not. I have no idea regarding Cecil, nor do I care. Maybe I say this because I peeked myself, now and then, not too often." Hernandez is unusual in his regard for peeking. "Is peeking cheating?" Hernandez asks himself in the book. "Absolutely not. Poor sportsmanship? No more than stealing signs or doctoring the ball. I consider all these tricks as part of the art and craft of playing baseball, not as cheating." On the other hand, Hernandez believes that hitting with a corked bat is cheating because there is no way of catching the trick on the field.

What is totally acceptable behavior by the batter is looking forward and picking up all one can. "The batter's obligation is to pick it up from what the pitcher is doing," said Cincinnati Reds hitting coordinator Leon Roberts. "Look at his glove. Is he fanning, changing his mechanics, changing his thing?"

If, on the other hand, a batter calls time because there is something in his eye and he steps back and looks down, he may be trying to get an idea of where the catcher is setting up and what pitch is being called. If this is an obvious attempt to peek—in violation of the unwritten rule against looking back—the next pitch is liable to be high and inside.

1.18.3. It Is Not a Player's Responsibility to Tell a Pitcher on His Own Team That He Is Tipping the Opposition to His Pitches through Unconscious Signs and Signals

Todd Jones, a candid observer of clubhouse mores, wrote this in his *Birmingham News* column of July 3, 2005: "One of the more intriguing unwritten rules of the game really doesn't make sense. Hitters will watch their own pitchers for tendencies, but won't tell them if they spot one. For instance, your teammate may flare his glove open while digging in for his curveball grip. Andy Benes always gritted his teeth when he was digging for a slider. When he was in Los Angeles, Hideo Nomo's hand was a different height for his fastball than for his split-finger." Jones asks and answers the obvious: "So why don't hitters help the pitchers on their own team? With trades and free agent movement today, players are often on different teams each year, and they want to keep an advantage if they have to face their former teammate. As a player gets older and begins to make his way out of the game, he may reveal more information. But most say absolutely nothing. It seems crazy that you would not let a pitcher on your team know inside information, but it rarely happens." Jones adds: "These are small tendencies, but they can prove devastating to a pitcher if the other team's batters know it. The Cardinals made Randy Johnson think that they had his pitches figured out. He went so far as to change his mechanics."

1.19.0. Rookies Are the
Lowest Rung on the Ladder

Pitcher Todd Jones, the modern player who has written most extensively on unwritten rules, says one of the best-known off-field unwritten rules is about rookies paying their dues. "For one thing, they learn quickly that the back of the plane and bus usually are designated for older players. Rookies usually wait until veterans have a seat and grab what's left. When they go to the clubhouse for water or gum during a game, they make a point of asking teammates if they need anything. They also have to play the pack mule, carrying stuff and doing whatever needs to be done. It's like the book *All I Really Need to Know I Learned in Kindergarten,* which emphasizes basic courtesy like respecting your elders."

The hierarchy even extends down to where rookies sit and sleep on buses in the minors. "We created our own little world on the bus," said pitcher Dallas Breden in 2005 after an exceptionally grueling twenty-one-day road trip by the Stockton Ports of the California League. "We have our hierarchy, and we have certain unwritten rules about where guys can sit. The older guys get to sit where they want and do what they want."

1.19.1. Rookies Are Supposed to Keep Their Mouths Shut and Pay Attention to Veterans and Coaches—Salaries Notwithstanding

"It is better to be seen than heard when you come up," said Don Mattingly when he was the New York Yankees' spring-training guest instructor. "You don't come up and talk too much. You come and listen. You got two ears and one mouth. You should listen twice as much as you talk."

1.20.0. Players Should Never Embarrass or Insult Umpires

1.20.1. A Batter Should Not "Show Up" an Umpire on a Ball-and-Strike Call

A batter is supposed to voice any complaints to the umpire without turning to look at him, thus not tipping off fans to the dispute and possibly turning the crowd against the umpire. Visiting hitters would turn the crowd in the ump's favor, but that would create the unseemly situation in which the umpire, by being cheered, had become an element in the game. You can break the rulebook rule about questioning ball-strike calls as long as you don't show that you are doing it. "Never turn around," John Mizerock, Kansas City Royals bullpen coach, said. "You can holler and pretty much say what you want as long as you are facing the pitcher."

1.20.2. A Pitcher Should Not "Show Up" an Umpire on a Ball-and-Strike Call

Tim Kurkjian has written: "As a pitcher, if an ump misses a pitch down the middle, do what Hall of Famer Fergie Jenkins used to do: don't even flinch, just keep on pitching. As good as umpires are, they're human. If you embarrass them, they'll embarrass you. They'll call you out on a bad pitch if you make them look bad."

1.20.3. Batters Are Allowed to Show Displeasure with an Umpire after a Called Third Strike by Shaking Their Head or Otherwise Showing Disbelief, but Throwing Things—Bat, Helmet, or Body Armor—Is Not Acceptable

"If you are hitting, as long as you don't look at the home-plate umpire or make any gestures toward him, he will listen to you," wrote pitcher Todd Jones in a 2001 article for *Sporting News* on dealing with umpires. "You can make a point and move on. It is a little trickier if you are a pitcher, because you are 60 feet away. You have to be more subtle. You can move your arms as if to ask where the pitch was. But you had better wait until the next day to ask him. Even then, he might not talk to you at all."

Jones asserted that post-millennium umpires are less confrontational and not looking for trouble. He also said that there were umpires who were confrontational and that dealing with them was akin to "handling snakes." Todd named the tough guys: Ken Kaiser, Joe West, Bruce Froemming, John Shulock, and Durwood Merrill. "If you talk to these guys like men and aren't demonstrative, you have a chance," writes Jones. But if you stop the flow of the game and draw attention to them or you, you're in trouble. "Umpires have gone through a complete change since I've been in the league. And things could not be better."

1.20.4. During an Argument with an Umpire, a Player Can Curse in Describing the Nature of the Call but Not to Characterize an Umpire

Every umpire has a "magic word" or words, the uttering of which guarantees ejection. "As you know, the baseball vocabulary can be terribly profane at times," says former major-league umpire Jim Evans, who operates the Jim Evans Academy of Professional Umpiring. "Many of the words are not objectionable to an umpire unless they are preceded by the personal pronoun 'you.' 'Sonofabitch' is okay. . . . 'you sonofabitch' is not. For example, no problem with 'Sonofabitch! I think you missed that!' However, one would be ejected for 'You sonofabitch! You missed that one!'" It is the same for the ten-letter words, he says, adding: You can get away with "That's a horseshit call!" but not "You're horseshit."

1.20.5. *NEVER* Is an Operative Word in Dealing with an Umpire unless You Are Angling for an Ejection

NEVER question the honesty or integrity of an umpire or his partner. NEVER show up the umpire by pulling out a rulebook to make your point. NEVER take first base on a three-ball count before the umpire has made his call. NEVER draw a line in the dirt with your foot.

1.20.6. Do Not Try to Deke the Umpire

A catcher who moves his glove after the ball hits it to a spot that will more likely get him the strike call and who is detected by the man in blue will not be happy with subsequent calls.

1.21.0. No Player Should Actually Take the Side of the Umpire Instead of His Teammate, Even if He Thinks the Umpire Is Correct

In August 2004, Jeff Bagwell actually sided with the call of the umpire to eject Roy Oswalt after he had drilled Michael

Barrett of the Cubs in the back. He said: "I would have done the same thing, I would have thrown Roy out. It was as blatant as it could be. That's it." Bagwell then went on to essentially question Oswalt's commitment to the team, because he got tossed and didn't provide enough innings of ace pitching skills.

This violation of two unspoken rules—siding with the ump and criticizing a teammate in public—caused Oswalt, a starter, to respond by offering to go in as reliever. He did get used in relief, and immediately won a game. An Astros blogger commenting on the story said: "That's the type of baseball story that makes the game interesting. It's all just a damn soap opera with sunflower seeds and statistics."

1.22.0. Decoying—Or Dekeing—Has an Important Place in Baseball

Decoying includes both the act of an offensive player deceiving a defensive player and the opposite, an act in which a defensive player deceives a base runner. An example of the former would be when a batter singles and acts as if he will stop at first base in order to trick the fielder into thinking the play is ending, at which point he breaks for second base.

Examples of the latter include luring the runner off his base with the hidden-ball trick; fielding a ball as though it will be misplayed; feinting the motions for a double play (when the batter hits a ball into the air or into the outfield), hoping that the runner will be decoyed into sliding or hesitating; confusing a runner so that he returns to a base; and standing at a base as though no throw is coming in, hoping the runner will slow up or not slide and thus can be tagged out. A rarer example would be for the second baseman to act in such a way as to entice the runner on first to try to steal.

1.22.1. Do Not Deke a Base Runner without Cause

Shortstops and second basemen sometimes try to fool base runners into thinking they should slide into second—behaving as if the batter hit a double-play grounder, when he actually hit one into the air or into the outfield. Thus deked, the runner wastes valuable time sliding.

"So why not 'deke' a runner just for the heck of it?" Ron Kroichick asked in an article on the unwritten rules published in the *San Francisco Chronicle* on May 12, 2000. His answer came from Giants hitting coach Gene Clines, who had been seething about this question for twenty-seven years. Clines, playing for Pittsburgh, was running from first base during a game against San Diego in 1973. The pitch was ball four. Padres second baseman Derrel Thomas inexplicably tried to deke Clines. Then, at the last moment, Thomas held up. Clines held up his slide, too—and tore ligaments in his right ankle. He was sidelined for six weeks and his ankle was never the same again. "The rest of my career, I tried to get [Thomas]," Clines said. "I never got the chance. It still pisses me off."

1.22.2. Do Not Deke or Otherwise Call Off a Defensive Player by Making a False Call

On May 30, 2007, in Toronto in the top of the ninth inning, the New York Yankees were leading the Blue Jays 7–5 with two outs. Alex Rodriguez, who was a runner on second base, broke for third on a Jorge Posada pop-up. As he came near Jays third baseman Howie Clark, A-Rod yelled something, and the ball dropped in for a run-scoring single.

Rodriguez later claimed that he yelled "Hah!" but Clark claimed that he yelled "Mine!" leading him to think it was a teammate calling him off the ball.

The truth of what he yelled will probably never be known, but regardless of what he actually screamed, the Blue Jays and baseball people in general saw this as a violation of the unwritten rules. Even Yankees manager Joe Torre admitted that he thought the ploy was inappropriate. "It's probably something he shouldn't have done," Torre said. "I don't sense he's going to do it again."

To be sure, the Yankees in general and Rodriguez in particular are publicity magnets. Yankees general manager Brian Cashman said the episode was blown out of proportion because of A-Rod's status as one of the game's most recognizable stars on its most storied team: "If this is in Kansas City, it probably would be a story that wouldn't have lasted two days. It's a longer story and louder story because it's New York and it's Alex Rodriguez."

1.22.3. A Player or Manager Should Use Any Dekes or Tricks He Can to Win

One of baseball's ironies is that violating the official rules by corking one's bat or doctoring a pitch is seen by players and managers as getting an edge, but violating an unwritten rule, such as showing up one's opponent, is seen as a serious transgression. "The tradition of professional baseball has been agreeably free of charity," wrote Heywood Broun in the *New*

York World in 1923, adding, "The rule is, 'Do anything you can get away with.'"

A fairly rare but relevant example is the old hidden-ball trick, which has a long history in the game. It is a time-honored legal ruse in which a baseman conceals the ball and hopes that the base runner believes it has been returned to the pitcher. When the runner steps off the base, he is summarily tagged out with the hidden ball. One of the classic versions of the hidden-ball trick came in 1958 when Chicago White Sox second baseman Nellie Fox asked Billy Gardner of the Baltimore Orioles to step off the bag for a moment while he cleaned it off. Gardner obliged and got tagged out by Fox.

As a Florida Marlin, Mike Lowell completed hidden-ball tricks in the back-to-back seasons of 2004 and 2005. Of the two, the most significant in terms of the outcome of the game took place on August 10, 2005, when he caught Luis Terrero of the Arizona Diamondbacks, who represented the tying run, as he took a lead off third in the eighth inning with Florida leading 6–5. Florida won the game 10–5.

Researcher Bill Deane has documented more than thirty examples of the play being executed. Today, it is uncommon in the majors but much more common in the minors and college baseball, where examples abound, including cases where faking a time-out is used to pull the runner off base.

But how far is too far? The Chicago Cubs complained furiously when, during a May 22, 2005, game, White Sox shortstop Juan Uribe tricked Cubs first baseman Derrek Lee by standing near second and signaling to Lee that a double down the first-base line by Jeromy Burnitz was foul. Specifically, Uribe held up his hands toward Lee as if to signal the ball was foul and he should stop running. Lee stopped at second, then made his way to third, but he would have scored without Uribe's intervention. Lee was stranded at third when Aramis Ramirez flied out to left, ending the inning.

The Cubs won the game 4–3, but complained long and bitterly about the first-inning deke. Lee laughed about the Uribe ploy after the game, but old-school Cubs manager Dusty Baker wasn't quite as jovial. He thought it violated unwritten baseball rules and could have resulted in an injury to his first baseman. "I guess that's gamesmanship, but that's not how we were taught to play," the Cubs' manager told Paul Sullivan of the *Chicago Tribune* after the game. "You don't tell a guy it's a foul ball unless it's a foul ball. That's not proper etiquette." White Sox manager Ozzie Guillen, alluding to the hidden ball trick, demurred: "That's the way we used to play the game."

Lee told Sullivan he was a "little bit" bothered that Uribe resorted to such tactics. "You don't tell someone it's foul unless it's foul," Lee said. "You get people hurt that way. I've seen a deke on the double play, but not telling [the runner] it's foul. It's part of the game, I guess. I should've been a little bit more aware and not fell for it."

The point at which such dekeing goes over all the lines is in the use of an extra baseball. Here, for example, is the beginning of an Associated Press story (June 26, 1964) about a Class-A New York-Pennsylvania League game at Bing-hamton, New York: "As a high fly hit by Dan Napoleon soared toward the fence last night, evidently bound for home run territory, it was suddenly snared from the air in a spectacular catch or so it appeared. But later, [Binghamton outfielder] John May . . . admitted he didn't catch the ball after all. He said he went through the gestures, but actually substituted a ball from his pocket for the one that was hit out of the park."

The story goes on to say that Napoleon was credited with a home run and the Binghamton team lost the game.

1.22.4. There Is a Thin Line
between Doctoring and Cheating

Pitcher Todd Jones, who has freely admitted using pine tar every time he pitched during his two years in Denver—at six thousand feet—insisted in one of his tell-all columns in the *Birmingham News* in June 2005 that "Pine tar is all around baseball. Everyone uses it in some way, like catchers who put it on their shin guards and infielders who put it on their gloves so the ball will stick. It's no big deal to most players." But he added quickly: "Vaseline and sandpaper are different. They're looked on as cheating, because they give too much of an advantage. Hitters have no chance if a pitcher knows how to use Vaseline or sandpaper."

Jones also says that the unwritten rule allows hitters to bone their bats—i.e., condensing the wood to make it harder by rubbing it against a bathroom sink, for instance—but that corking one's bat is cheating. Hitters bone their bats in broad daylight because it's not considered cheating. "If pitchers find out a guy is corking, he's a marked man."

2.0.0. The Unwritten Rules for Managing—Also Known as "The Book"

In the seventh game of a hypothetical World Series, the team you manage has a two-run lead in the bottom of the ninth. Your opponent has two outs and men on first and second with the team's best hitter coming to the plate.

There is no question as to what you, the manager, have to do.

You have to pitch to the slugger, because "The Book" is very clear on this point. What is The Book?

It is an unwritten and ever-refined compendium of conventional wisdom, strategic thought, intuitive impulses, and time-tested axioms that define how the game of baseball should be managed; the collection of assumptions and percentages used to make on-field decisions; the accumulated baseball knowledge "of the ages." These unwritten but widely observed "rules" have "served as silent mentor to every manager who ever decided to go for the win on the road or play for a tie at home" (Peter Schmuck, *Baltimore Sun*, July 24, 2002). Perhaps the most often-cited example of a tenet of "The Book" is that during crucial at bats and when selecting pinch hitters or relief pitchers, left-handed batters face right-handed pitchers and vice versa. The obverse is true when selecting a relief pitcher—bring in a left-handed pitcher to face a left-handed batter and right-handed pitcher to face a right-handed batter. The idea here is to allow the manager to manipulate his substitutions to create situational advantages.

Other tenets include never intentionally walk the potential winning run; don't make the first or third out at third base; never throw behind the runner; don't use the closer in a tie game; hit to the right side with a runner at first base; and don't play the infield in early in the game. A manager who makes an unconventional move is said to be "going against The Book." But he is apt to respond, "He who lives by The Book can also die by The Book."

Advocates of established practices and conventions—those who adhere to the unwritten rules of baseball—generally attract the label of "old school." "Jim Leyland is as old school as they come, a baseball traditionalist who wears his spikes all day," wrote Chris Ballard in *Sports Illustrated* (August 21, 2006). The term implies maturity, leadership, aggressiveness, intensity, lack of foolishness, a no-nonsense style.

The Book's tenets range from the bone simple to the arcane and describe everything from the proper way of running the bases to the order in which hitters are slotted in the batting order.

2.1.0. Never Intentionally Put the Winning Run on Base

To walk this batter—even if the man on deck is statistically less likely to get a hit—and end up losing the game would be widely seen as pure folly. To go against The Book is to go against the holy writ of the game, which has been around since the first managers professed allegiance to a code of basic baseball strategy. It is based on principles that "everyone knows" are reliable and true and is very real in the sense that its assumptions and tenets are used to make many basic baseball decisions.

Despite this, The Book prompts a healthy skepticism. "Number one, I don't know who wrote The Book and none of us have actually ever seen The Book," said former Chicago

Cubs manager Dusty Baker. A few have flaunted it openly, as manager Dick Williams noted almost twenty-five years ago: "I never play by The Book because I never met the guy that wrote it." Some writers and long-term observers of the game are disdainful of The Book: "Guys who manage by The Book are guys who are afraid of losing their jobs," said Tracy Ringolsby of Denver's *Rocky Mountain News*.

The Book is also very well known by the fans and media, who are quick to criticize when a skipper goes against The Book and fails. "Very few managers are willing to go against The Book just in case it backfires," said veteran baseball writer Paul White of *USA Today Sports Weekly*. Some managers, on the other hand, insist that a prime function of The Book is to give the media something by which to judge managers. "If you play by The Book, it will keep the writers from getting on you for not playing by The Book" is what Seattle manager Bob Melvin said in 2003, his first year on the job, "but it will also limit your options."

Baseball history contains many examples of managers who have gone against The Book and failed. When Joe Torre was managing the New York Mets in the late 1970s, he walked the potential go-ahead run (Bill Buckner) in back-to-back games at Wrigley Field, and both times he watched as his pitcher gave up a home run to the next batter (Dave Kingman), whom he thought would be the easier out. "But to me," Torre recently told the *Baltimore Sun*, "Buckner was a better hitter. I got crucified for it, but I never second-guessed myself."

2.2.0. Never Intentionally Walk in a Run, but Never, Ever Walk in the Potential Winning Run

The most exciting modern casebook example of this unwritten rule about walking in the potential winning run being flaunted took place on May 28, 1998, when Buck Showalter's Arizona Diamondbacks led the San Francisco Giants 8–6 with two outs in the bottom of the ninth and the bases loaded. Barry Bonds came to the plate, where he was served four straight balls, intentionally walking in a run, putting the tying run on third and the winning run on second. San Francisco catcher Brent Mayne was up next, and on a 3–2 count he lined out to right field to end the game and validated Showalter's exceedingly uncommon move, which had been made only three times previously in the twentieth century.

(Research conducted by Bill Deane and Everett Parker and published in the November 2003 *Baseball Digest* could find only three hitters who had been walked intentionally in the same situation prior to the Bonds incident in 1998: Napoleon Lajoie, on May 23, 1901; Del Bissonette, on May 2, 1928; and Bill Nicholson, on July 23, 1944. In all three cases, the manager who called for the intentional run won the game. In the case of the Lajoie incident, the Philadelphia Athletics were batting against the Chicago White Sox in the top of the ninth. Behind 11–7 with the bases loaded and no outs and with Lajoie, on his way to a Triple Crown, at bat, Sox manager Clark Griffith inserted himself as a relief pitcher and deliberately walked Lajoie. Griffith then disposed of Socks Seybold, Harry Davis, and Morgan Murphy, all on infield grounders, to preserve the 11–8 win.)

Showalter got away with that bold decision, but most baseball managers would think long and hard before going so far against the accumulated baseball knowledge of the ages. "There were about fifteen variables that would never come up again," said Showalter in a spring-training interview in 2003 as first-year manager of the Texas Rangers. "Bonds had come in in a double switch, so he didn't have Jeff Kent behind him. Mayne was a good major-league player, but he was no Jeff Kent. I only had one pitcher left. It was raining. The ground was wet and there were about ten other variables. . . . We had a good chance to win a game, but not with Barry Bonds hitting. I felt very strongly that if he hit in that situation, the game was over. Then we got lucky. It could also have gone the other way." "Mayne really hit that ball hard," observed Tracy Ringolsby, veteran baseball writer for the *Rocky Mountain News*. "If that was a gapper it would have been a stupid move."

The other factor at work that night was that Bonds is often cited as the prime example of why it sometimes is acceptable to put the go-ahead run on base. "I think that Barry Bonds has completely destroyed The Book in many ways," said Tim Kurkjian of ESPN in 2001. "I've been covering baseball for almost 25 years and never seen a guy intentionally walked with no one on base and I've seen Barry walked 19 times in that situation."

2.3.0. Never Make the First or Last Out of an Inning at Third Base

As explained by Johnny Bench in *The Complete Idiot's Guide to Baseball* (1999): "In other words, don't try to steal third, or go from first to third on a single, or push a double into a triple, with no outs or two outs." Examples of violations of this law abound. Red Sox slugger Manny Ramirez ended an inning by being put out at third early in Game 3 of the 2004 ALCS. The Yankees were ahead, 3–0, en route to a 19–8 win and a 3–0 series lead. Stealing third is often inappropriate (even though it is easier to steal third than to steal second) because a single usually scores a runner from second. The modern application of this axiom may also explain why batters in past eras tended to have more triples, because it limits the times the batter can try to turn a solid double into a questionable triple. Making the second out at third is not a good idea, either, but at least it doesn't have the same rally-snuffing effect as the first or third out.

In an interview in *Fortune,* Joe Torre told about Derek Jeter violating this unwritten rule and how it almost caused the low-key skipper to uncharacteristically lose his temper. "He's a rookie. He's at second base against the White Sox in Chicago, we're in the top of the eighth inning, we're losing by a run. Now, there's an unwritten rule in baseball that you never make the first or last out at third base. [There are two outs], and Cecil Fielder's the hitter—one of our big boppers—and all of a sudden I see Jeter taking off for third. It's a bad play if you're out. And he gets thrown out. . . . So I'm throwing clipboards and all that, which is very uncharacteristic of me, because I don't want to watch myself on ESPN for a week on end throwing shit in the dugout. [So] I said to Zimmer, sitting next to me, 'I'm not going to talk to him about this until tomorrow, because I don't want to rattle him today.'"

2.4.0. Right-Handed Pitchers Have a Better Chance of Retiring Right-Handed Batters and Lefties Are More Successful against Lefties

By extension, The Book says you don't bring a right-handed reliever in to face a left-handed batter but, by the same token, with a right-hander on the mound, you don't walk a right-handed batter to pitch to a lefty.

But all of this is subject to a reality check. "People would stack their lineups with righties against Tom Glavine," said Milwaukee skipper Ned Yost, a longtime Atlanta Braves coach. "You were playin' right into his hands. As a left-handed pitcher he was far more effective against righties than lefties."

2.5.0. You Should Meet Strength with Strength; Concede Nothing

This obtains from the first day of the season, even if your team is predicted to lose a hundred games. It also comes into play when a seemingly inferior team goes up against a team heading for the postseason. By conceding nothing, the lowly 2007 Florida Marlins went on a roll that ultimately bumped the New York Mets out of the play-off picture.

2.6.0. As a General Rule, the Batting Lineup Consists of the "Table Setters," the "Sluggers," and the "Bottom of the Lineup"

The Book describes the order in which the hitters appear at the plate to optimize the team's chances for scoring runs. The batting order is very deliberately chosen by a team, and new players are acquired and existing players are traded away, in part, based on the order in which they will appear. Casey Stengel was once asked whom he would choose to lead off his batting order and where he would place his big hitters. "In the middle of your order," he declared as part of his contribution to The Book, "you should never have two slow-footed, right-handed sluggers battin' one after the other, because the double plays will murder you."

2.7.0. Don't Go against "the Percentages"

The bulk of The Book is a list of commonsense prohibitions: don't issue an intentional walk if first base is occupied; don't make the first or third out at third base; don't hit and run when the count is 0–2; don't go against the percentages; don't bring in your closer and don't bring the infield in or straddle the lines during the early innings of a game. These are all based on good common sense. No manager would normally play his infield in during the early innings of a tight game, because the benefits of avoiding a single run at the plate are clearly outweighed by the possibility that a hit through the infield could lead to multiple runs. But suppose the opposing pitcher is a Sandy Koufax or Randy Johnson working at his overpowering best, and your gut says that one run might decide who wins the game. This is where certain managers might consider going against The Book.

The Book also says that you bring the infield in under certain circumstances, such as protecting a lead late in the game. But not everyone agrees with this. Casey Stengel once pointed out that bringing the infield in turns a .200 hitter into a .300 hitter.

The Book also says that you should always guard the lines in certain late-inning situations. "I've seen a lot of games lost because everyone goes by The Book and puts their players on the lines in the late innings to protect a lead," said Anaheim Angels coach Mickey Hatcher. "I have also seen a lot of games won by going against The Book and playing from the normal defensive position, especially with batters who hit down the middle." Hatcher, who has reservations about The Book, adds, "Mike Scioscia doesn't always go by The Book, and we won a World Championship because he does take chances."

Significantly, both managers in the 2002 World Series have reputations as being able go against The Book when their gut—or instinct, as many call it—tells them to override The Book. "The Book is just a commonsense reference to what your team needs; but there are many ways to accomplish what The Book says should be done," said Mike Scioscia, manager of the 2002 World Champion Anaheim Angels, during spring training in 2003. "I think there are times when you should put the winning run on base, if you feel that the percentages of getting the next hitter out are incredibly in your favor . . . It boils down to what I need to do to win the game; not what I don't want to do to try not to lose the game."

When asked if he plays by The Book, Scioscia's 2002 World Series opponent, Dusty Baker, who was with the Chicago Cubs in 2003, replied: "It depends on who you are playing, depends on the score. The scoreboard dictates everything, so sometimes you have to go against The Book, but when you go against The Book you leave yourself open for second-guessing if it doesn't work." He added, "But if it does work, then you're a great manager."

Just as some of the most well-established managers are willing to depart from The Book, so, too, are some of those in their first full seasons as skippers—a trend that suggests more, not less, unconventional moves in the future. "As far as The Book is concerned, I will gamble. The same situation will come up twice, and I may handle it two different ways," said Ned Yost, speaking as rookie manager of the Milwaukee Brewers in 2003, who seems to relish the notion of unpredictability and sees precedent in the history of the game. "Leo Durocher did things that were completely off-the-wall, totally against The Book. People asked him why and he said that he didn't want anyone to have any idea what he was doing at any time. Totally unpredictable." As a freshman skipper in Seattle, Bob Melvin said, "There is a book, but I'm not the kind of guy who is going to be hampered by it." Clint Hurdle of the Colorado Rockies said, "I don't manage by The Book, I manage by the gut more than The Book." Entering his first full season as a major-league manager in 2002, Hurdle added, "I actually like the Cliff Notes on The Book better than I like The Book itself."

2.8.0. Show Patience

2.9.0. Promote from Within

2.10.0. Contend, Not Just for One Season, but for a Succession of Seasons

2.11.0. Managers Should Not Criticize Their Teams, No Matter How Badly They Perform

However, this rule does not extend to criticism by owners. "There is an unwritten rule that managers cannot criticize a team," Yankees owner George Steinbrenner was quoted widely in 1980 as saying, "but an owner sure as hell can, because he's the one who signs the paychecks."

2.12.0. The Manager Should Remain Detached from His Players to Maintain Their Respect

This rule is long established and ratified through most of the twentieth century. "A manager should stay as far away as possible from his players," advised Baltimore Orioles skipper Earl Weaver after his induction into the Baseball Hall of Fame in 1996. "I don't know if I said ten words to Frank Robinson while he played for me." Robinson played for Weaver from 1968 through 1971.

Some managers still observe this, but others have chosen to abandon it. "Not getting close to your players is a mistake," says St. Louis Cardinals skipper Tony La Russa. "You spend eight months together. It's pretty much like your family in that you can tell somebody that they have done something wrong and still be respected."

2.12.1. Managers of Teams out of Contention Play Regular Players against Contending Teams out of Respect for Other Contenders

3.0.0. The Unwritten Rules for Umpires

The official rules for the umpire are extremely specific up to and including the admonition "Keep your eye everlastingly on the ball while it is in play." But even this is superseded by certain unwritten rules that say, for example, that the first-base umpire never watches the ball, but watches the feet of the first baseman and the feet of the runner. He calls the play based on the popping sound the ball makes in the first baseman's glove.

3.1.0. Umpires Will Permit "Neighborhood Play" to Avoid Mayhem on the Bases

During an attempted double play, the umpire will call a base runner out if the man covering second or third has his foot near the base, rather than on it, to avoid an incoming slide. This is also known as the "phantom tag." The umpire only rules an out when the toss is on target, the ball is caught cleanly, and the fielder's foot is in the vicinity of the bag. This is not what the rulebook says (rule 7.08 says the fielder must touch the bag or make the tag), and the play is never formally acknowledged by the higher-ups in baseball. There is a reason for this unwritten rule that is intensely practical. "Historians say the rough-and-tumble play of the 1930s led to the 'phantom tag' call. Following the letter of the law resulted in too many collisions, fights and injuries," wrote Kirk Arnott in an article on the neighborhood play in the *Columbus Dispatch* early in the 1992 baseball season. "In these days of fragile millionaires, can you imagine how swollen the disabled list would be if the phantom tag wasn't called? There already are more than 90 guys on the disabled list, and it's only April."

3.2.0. Umpires Don't Fight or Complain; They Punish

Umpires have been known to change the strike zone for pitchers who have embarrassed them and to make bad calls to retaliate for a player's dissatisfaction with a particular call at the plate.

3.3.0. Umpires Must Always
Protect Each Other

3.3.1. No Matter What Your Opinion Is of
Another Umpire, Never Make an Adverse
Comment Regarding Him

"To do so is despicable and ungentlemanly" is what former baseball commissioner Ford C. Frick once specified about any umpire who violated this unwritten rule.

3.4.0. Umpires Never Let Players
See Them Wince

Umpires don't "take a knee," that is, kneel in response to pain. And they don't ever end up flat on their backs unless they are gravely injured.

3.4.1. Catchers Cover for Umpires Who
Need a Few Moments to Recover

It's a fairly standard practice for a catcher to go to the mound and stall after an umpire gets hit with a foul ball. I think umps and catchers are in the same boat with regard to foul tips and make every effort to let the other know if there is a problem that might need a few extra moments of recovery time.

3.5.0. Umpires Do Not Fraternize with Players and Coaches

The official rules of the game state that "Umpires, on the field, should not indulge in conversation with players. Keep out of the coaching box and do not talk to the coach on duty." This does not mean they cannot talk to players and coaches, and they do. On the subject, former MLB umpire Jim Evans says: "Some umpires do it more than others. In my opinion, an umpire should not initiate conversation but be professional and courteous if addressed. If a player or coach leaves his position and comes to the umpire, it is only natural for the umpire to respond to a question or greeting. The major objection to fraternization is when the umpire leaves his position to initiate the exchange."

Evans, who served as a crew chief for almost twenty years, gave this advice to his crews: "Be professional and courteous but not solicitous. Don't get a reputation as a politician. The person you are trying to befriend in one inning may be the guy you have to eject the next. Strive for respect with your work; not popularity with your BS."

Do umpires ever admit to a bad call on the field? It happens. "I'm not too proud to admit I have made a mistake," umpire Dick Urlage told a reporter for the *Cincinnati Post* in 1991. "A catcher may turn and say to me, 'That was a strike.' And I may . . . say, 'You better believe that was a heck of a pitch. I called it too quickly.' Usually, that's the end of it."

3.5.1. Don't Socialize with Club Personnel off the Field; Don't Hang Out in the Club Dressing Room or Administrative Offices

Umpiring teams hang out with their fellow members, but not with coaches and players. Exceptions are few and far between. National League umpire Joe West once invited San Francisco Giants infielder/outfielder Ryan Klesko to a country-western-themed golf tournament. Klesko loved it, and the two have been swapping invitations ever since. It has made news, because the two broke, as the *Atlanta Journal-Constitution* put it, the unwritten baseball taboo by furthering a player-ump friendship.

3.6.0. The Best Umpire Is an Invisible Umpire—If You Are Conspicuous, You Are Not Doing a Good Job

The fact is that in recent years it has been easier for umpires to maintain a low profile. "I think that the personalities in the game are different than a few years ago," says Jim Evans, who directs the Jim Evans Academy of Professional Umpiring. "Guys like Billy Martin, Earl Weaver, and Dick Williams were constantly challenging umpires and initiating confrontations. Many of these confrontations got vicious and became personal attacks on the umpires. Many of the managers who managed against these guys felt they had to be more aggressive or the umpires would be intimidated. Untrue, of course, but it was a perception among some. The umpires often fought back and, of course, this made for good TV."

Evans also points out that the umpiring crews tend to be younger men today and that they have been indoctrinated into taking a more docile approach to handling certain situations. They have an evaluation system that determines who is assigned special events, and this encourages the umpires to avoid as much controversy as possible. "Many umpires today are striving to stay below the radar."

The irony here is that there have been eight umpires whose outstanding work was visible enough to earn them entry into the National Baseball Hall of Fame.

3.7.0. The Umpire Has the Right to Eject a Player, Coach, or Manager from a Game

Technically, this is also a written rule, but unwritten rules come into play. There are well-kept stats on ejections that become a major part of the reputation of players and, more often, managers. On September 21, 2007, during the eighth inning in a Braves game against the Milwaukee Brewers, Bobby Cox was ejected for the 133rd time, an all-time record. The record was previously held by the fierce John McGraw with 131, some of which he earned as a player. Third baseman Arlie Latham, who played in seventeen seasons from 1880 to 1909 for six major-league teams, said that McGraw "eats gunpowder every morning and washes it down with warm blood."

3.7.1. Umpires Have "Magic Words"
That Virtually Guarantee an Ejection

There are two major magic words. One contains twelve letters. The other has ten.

If a batter utters a profanity after striking out, he will probably remain in the game. But if a batter turns to the umpire and directs the profanity at him, the player will be ejected. Adding "you" to a vulgarism usually means ejection.

3.7.2. Trying to Show Up the Umpire
Is Cause for Ejection

For example, if a catcher holds his glove over the plate when a pitch is called a ball, he will usually be warned not to try to frame the ball again. A repeat of the action can lead to ejection. "I have told more than one catcher, 'You frame that ball again in an effort to show me up and you're out of here,'" umpire Dick Urlage said in an article on the unwritten rules of ejection that appeared in the *Cincinnati Post* in 1991.

3.7.3. Any Action Designed to Incite the Crowd against the Umpire Is Cause for Ejection

Throwing equipment is at the top of the list. This falls under the heading of "showing up" an umpire. Among the most memorable ejections listed by Gerry Fraley in the September 2007 *Baseball Digest* is one in which the point of inciting the crowd was well underscored: "On April 27, 1983, Seattle manager Rene Lachemann literally begged to be ejected. He explained to the umpiring crew that erratic owner George Argyros would be pacified if Lachemann were ejected. Steve Palermo complied, and Lachemann tossed a few batting helmets onto the field for extra effect. However, Lachemann forgot that it was Batting Helmet Night at the Kingdome, and the giveaway items soon sailed out of the seats."

3.7.4. A Manager Who Overstays His Welcome in Discussing a Disputed Call Will Be Ejected

The umpire will let a manager have his say, but will signal that the conversation is over and any more talking will bring on an ejection by turning away.

3.7.5. A Manager Who Brings a Rulebook onto the Field or Cites a Television Replay in a Confrontation with the Umpire Will Be Tossed

On June 1, 2007, Bobby Abreu of the New York Yankees was thrown out trying to steal third against Boston. During a Red Sox pitching change later in the inning, Yankees manager Joe Torre told umpire Jerry Crawford the television replay showed Abreu was actually safe. Crawford ejected Torre.

3.8.0. The Major Operative Verb for Umpires Is "Don't"

"Don't treat superstars any different than rookies" and "Don't let personalities affect your work" are two "don'ts" that Jim Evans uses when instructing in his umpiring academy. But there are others. While discussing how umpires should do their job, the late John McSherry once said: "There are only two real no-nos. You must keep your head out of the dugout (not worrying about the bench jockeys), and you don't stand around looking for some player who wants to say something." But there are more. Hall of Fame umpire Bill McGowan listed twenty-five "don'ts," which he used in his Florida school for umpires (they are all listed with his comments as Appendix C). Among the most salient: "Don't call your plays too quickly," "Don't explain your decisions," "Don't take your eyes off the pitcher once he steps on that rubber," "Don't turn away from a play too quickly," and "Don't fail to call interference plays immediately."

4.0.0. The Unwritten Rules for the Official Scorer

4.1.0. The Official Scorer Should Make Sure That the First Hit of a Game Is a Good One When There Is Even the Slight Chance That the Pitcher Is In the Early Stages of a No-hitter

This unwritten rule has been in effect for many years, has a long history of having been observed, and, according to scorekeeping expert Andy Wirkmaa, is observed at all levels of the game. Occasionally, someone will step forth and challenge this unwritten rule, but such occurrences are few and far between.

One who crusaded against it was Dick Young, the powerful and often irascible reporter for the *New York Daily*

News (and later the *New York Post*), who was quoted in *Sporting News* in 1953 calling this a "gutless approach." He asked why a hit in the third inning should be an error in the ninth. "At the risk of sounding like Gertie Stein: a hit is a hit is a hit. It shouldn't matter when, or by whom, or under what circumstances."

4.2.0. When It Comes to the Official Scorekeeping, Unwritten Rules over Time Often Become Written

Andy Wirkmaa, author of *Baseball Scorekeeping: A Practical Guide to the Rules,* on the most recent example, in an e-mail sent to the author:

For many years, there was an unwritten rule in scorekeeping that (by virtue of the 2007 MLB revisions) has become a written rule. Specifically, before 2007, when a fielder abandoned or otherwise discarded a live ball in play, erroneously believing that three outs had been logged, and a runner or runners advanced as a result of that fact, the official scorer was faced with a real problem: The rulebook stated that "Mental mistakes or misjudgments are not to be scored as errors unless specifically covered in the rules" [see "old" Rule 10.13: Note (3)] and flipping the ball into the stands, or handing the ball to an umpire and walking away, or anything like that was not one of the very few "mental errors" that were listed in the rulebook as mistakes that constituted official fielding errors.

Consequently, because altogether undesirable and erroneous repercussions would arise if the official scorer did not consider the fielder's blunder in cases like this as being a fielding error, official scorers would contrive some sort of subterfuge (like deeming the fielder's handing the ball to the blonde with large breasts wearing a tank top in the first row a "wild throw") and ascribe the ramifications of the fielder's "brain freeze" to an error (when, in fact, no error was technically committed).

But that was then.

Now we have . . . the pronouncement that "A fielder's mental mistake that leads to a physical misplay—such as throwing the ball into the stands or rolling the ball to the pitcher's mound, mistakenly believing there to be three outs, and thereby allowing a runner or runners to advance—shall not be considered a mental mistake for purposes of this rule and the official scorer shall charge a fielder committing such a mistake with an error."

5.0.0. The Unwritten Rules for Fans

5.1.0. In Areas That Have Two Baseball Teams, Any Given Fan Can Only Really Root for One of Them

This is truer in certain places than others, but it's certainly most accurate in Chicago and New York, followed by the San Francisco–Oakland Bay area and the Los Angeles–Anaheim area. It is most tenuous in the newly crafted Baltimore-Washington area, but this game is still in the early innings.

5.2.0. Never Accept Coins from a Vendor

Let 'em keep that change or your row will brand you as a cheapskate.

5.3.0. Don't Throw Anything on the
Field . . . Except an Opponent's Home Run Ball

Under certain circumstances, it is right and proper to throw back a ball that has been hit into the stands by a hated opponent. The tradition of tossing a visitor's ball back appears to have begun with the partisan bleacherites at Wrigley Field in the 1980s. In the mid-1980s, Bob Wood could report in his book *Dodger Dogs to Fenway Franks* that it was "a ritual practiced by no other group of fans in the majors." Wood was able to report this after touring all twenty-six major-league parks during the summer of 1985. But now it has been reported elsewhere.

"Personally, I would never do that," says Zack Hample, the self-described "professional fan" who at the beginning of 2008 had snagged 3,277 balls from forty-two major-league ballparks. "I'd rather get beat up than part with a home run ball, but then again, knowing the tradition that exists at Wrigley, I wouldn't be stupid enough to sit out there. Then again, fans out there are famous for keeping 'dummy balls' in their pockets and throwing THOSE back instead of the real home runs. I think it's up to the individual fan, but yeah, it's a great tradition. If you're gonna throw a ball back, though, you have to do it the right way. Otherwise, you risk injuring a player, delaying the game, and getting ejected by security. You just have to be smart about it."

5.4.0. The Relationship between the Fan and the Foul Ball Is as Much a Part of Baseball as Peanuts and Cracker Jack

There was a time when fans were required to return foul balls. The Cubs were the first to allow fans to keep the balls in 1916. But it took many years for all teams to regard the balls as anything other than stolen property. In 1923, the Phillies had an eleven-year-old boy arrested for keeping a foul ball. The boy spent the night in prison, and he became a local hero when he came out of prison as a fan of the Philadelphia Athletics. The boy became part of Phillies lore invoked in 2007 at the time of the ten-thousandth loss in the team's history, as part of the disdain that certain fans had for the team's management eighty-four years later.

5.5.0. Root for the Visiting Team
at Your Own Risk

Professional fan and baseball author Zack Hample puts it this way: "If you root for the visiting team, you WILL get verbally abused, and if you're in Yankee Stadium, you'll get physically abused as well." There are now major exceptions to this rule. Red Sox fans who have trouble getting Fenway tickets sometimes come down to Baltimore in such great numbers that it seems like a Boston home game. The same can be true with some Philadelphia games in D.C.

5.6.0. Baseball Fans Have a Long-Established
and Inalienable Right to Throw Peanut Shells
and Other Litter Around Their Seats

Hample again: "It's one of the pleasures of being at a baseball game . . . getting to litter. Without littering, those poor people on the cleaning crew wouldn't have jobs. Then again, if they didn't have jobs, ticket prices would be lower. But really, I say it's fine to litter IN the seats. Not in the concourses or bath-rooms, et cetera."

Another Hample tip: "Fans should tip the usher if he (or she) wipes off the seats with a rag that ISN'T dirtier than the seat itself."

5.7.0. Keeping Score Allows for Personal Interpretation, but There Are Unwritten Protocols That Must Be Observed

The most important of these are the use of K as the symbol for a strikeout and the numbering of defensive players. Here is the immutable order of scoring.

POSITION	ABBREVIATION	SCORECARD NUMBER
Pitcher	P	1
Catcher	C	2
First baseman	1B	3
Second baseman	2B	4
Third baseman	3B	5
Shortstop	SS	6
Left fielder	LF	7
Center fielder	CF	8
Right fielder	RF	9

6.0.0. The Unwritten Rules for the Media
and for Dealing with Same

6.1.0. There Are Unwritten Rules
for the Media

Reporters with official credentials are subject to a strict code, both written and unwritten, which—as with so many other aspects of the game—has its own personality. Newspapers and baseball enjoyed a parallel history in America, with one feeding the other. As Connie Mack once wrote: "It has been affirmed that tens of millions read the news on the sporting pages every day. From these come the vast crowds that witness the game." The symbiosis of ink and baseball has been unparalleled and only rivaled by boxing and horse racing in the early days of newspapers.

Beat writers and columnists wrote about more than one sport, but the reputations of the likes of Red Smith, Grantland Rice, the Lardners, Fred Lieb, and Shirley Povich were built on baseball reporting.

Baseball was made for radio and vice versa. With the advent of broadcasting came some new unwritten rules and taboos, including the provision about not mentioning a no-hitter in progress. However, the most puzzling unwritten rule in the early days of broadcasting baseball was one which—for reasons now obscured by time—prohibited the use of the word *blood* in the context of a baseball game. In the days following the 1941 Japanese attack on Pearl Harbor, Brooklyn Dodgers broadcaster Red Barber was approached by the man in charge of recruiting blood donors in the borough about helping in the effort to attract volunteers because of a desperate blood shortage in the nation. Barber told him about the unwritten rule and said he could not approve the request. Barber went to fellow redhead and Dodgers major-domo Larry MacPhail, who responded gruffly, "Hell, men are dying because they need blood."

6.1.1. Access to the Press Box Is Strictly Limited

Each team and every league at all levels of play reserve the press box for those with closely guarded credentials.

6.1.2. There Is No Cheering in the Press Box

Nor can you clap, whistle, or pump your fist in the air. "They sit politely, like once-removed cousins at the reading of the will," wrote Mark Taylor, a general assignment reporter for the *Indiana Post-Tribune* on a 1989 visit to the press box at Wrigley Field. "Like the shy guys at an orgy." He added that in a baseball press box, "the only excitement comes when a new entree is announced in the cafeteria."

"The biggest drawback to sitting in the press box is you're not allowed to cheer" was the response when Joe Dirck, a political reporter for the *Cleveland Plain Dealer,* was temporarily assigned to the Indians' press box in 1995. "It's sort of an unwritten rule among sportswriters. I forgot a couple of times and started to clap when the Tribe did something good. People turned around and glared at me as if I had a case of the giggles at a state funeral. Sorry."

One of the reasons why access to the press box is guarded with such zeal is to protect against those who do not understand the rule. This unwritten rule is true of all major sports. A violation that made the news came in 1991 when rap star M. C. Hammer was chided for cheering Deion Sanders from the Atlanta Falcons press box. When he broke the rule the second time in the wake of a Deion interception, he looked around sheepishly and told the assembled writers, "Somebody's going to have to write down that unwritten rule."

Then there was the incident in 1989 during a series in St. Louis, when a man wearing a Cardinals jersey stood in a section reserved for the San Francisco writers and began to cheer for the Cardinals.

"I'm sorry, sir, there's no cheering allowed in the press box," said Duffy Jennings, the Giants' vice president of public relations. "This is a working area."

"When I'm in my home stadium, I'll cheer the home team," the man said.

"Do you belong here?" Jennings asked.

"I belong wherever I want to be," the man said.

After a few more angry exchanges, during which the man identified himself, he turned and left, displaying the name ASHCROFT on the back of his jersey—that was John D. Ashcroft, governor of Missouri and future attorney general.

This is not to say that there has never been cheering in the press box. Veteran writer Hal McCoy of the *Dayton Daily News* said in the 2001 History Channel documentary *Baseball: Stories from the Press Box* that when Pete Rose collected hit number 4,192 to surpass Ty Cobb, "the press box exploded . . . that's the first time I ever saw that."

6.1.3.In All Baseball Press Boxes, There Is a Prohibition against Commenting on How Quickly a Game Is Proceeding

"Even if the first eight innings are finished in fewer than 2 hours," wrote Drew Olsen in the *Milwaukee Journal Sentinel* back in 1996, "you keep your mouth shut out of fear. The theory, which has been proved countless times, holds that as soon as somebody says 'Boy, this game is really flying' the pace will grind to a halt and everyone will be subjected to a string of pitching changes, agonizingly long innings and possibly a weather delay or power failure."

6.1.4. A Press Pass Allows One into the Clubhouse but Does Not Allow One to Poke Around in a Player's Locker or Enumerate What Is in That Locker

In 1998, the Colorado Rockies filed a complaint with the National League office to have action taken against a *Denver Post* columnist who was seen taking a bottle of androstenedione, Mark McGwire's muscle enhancer of choice, from Dante Bichette's locker. Bichette at this time was a national spokesperson for a company that produced similar nutritional supplements. The reporter lost his press credentials. Rockies manager Don Baylor told a reporter: "I've been a player, coach and manager, and that's one of those things that's an unwritten rule. You don't go into a guy's locker."

6.1.5. The Seating in the Press Box Follows a Careful Pecking Order

The first row is reserved for members of the Baseball Writers Association of America (BBWA). There are also rules of seniority. Peter Schmuck, of the *Baltimore Sun* and a recent president of the BBWA, says that this tradition is so strong that if Cal Ripken Jr. chose to sit in Schmuck's seat in the front row of the press box at Camden Yards, he could be ordered out.

6.1.6. The Press Box Is Ruled by a Steward Who Settles All Disputes

This position is determined by convention in each press box and is based on the role played by a shop steward on the floor of a factory. The steward is also the official press liaison with the team.

6.1.7. Other Members of the Media Stand Back from Any One-on-One Interview with a Player, Coach, or Manager

Violation of this rule often results in a shoving match.

6.1.8. Sharing Is Not a Virtue in the Press Box

This rule dates back to a time when small cities had two newspapers, larger cities had a half dozen or more, and baseball stories were filed around the clock during the season. In such an environment, the urge to share with all was nil, and it still is. There are not as many newspapers today, but the competition—among radio, broadcast television, cable, and dot-commers—is still fierce.

6.1.9. Journalists Still Don't Write about the Private Peccadilloes of Ballplayers, but the Unwritten Rule Is Eroding

"STRAY-ROD" blared the page 1 headline in the tabloid *New York Post* across a picture of New York Yankees star Alex Rodriguez and an unidentified woman in Toronto on May 30, 2007. "Alex hits strip club with mystery blonde," it continued, and an inside headline rubbed it in harder: A-ROD'S A YANKEE DOODLE RANDY—HITS A STRIP JOINT WITH TORONTO BABE. Many felt that the newspaper had violated the unwritten rule, and Yankees manager Joe Torre agreed: "When you get into that area, I think it's over the line. It's what people seem to think is important or seem to think they have to do." There was a time when excessive drinking and behavior such as being "beaned up" on greenies (amphetamines) was protected. So was a fight in the clubhouse or a dispute on the team plane or bus, but this is eroding. Virtually every reporter covering Mickey Mantle and Billy Martin knew that these men had drinking problems, but it was protected information. *Baltimore Sun* reporter Peter Schmuck believes the rule began to erode in September 1984, following disclosures in a federal court in Pittsburgh that thirteen Major League Baseball players had been habitual users of cocaine. The Pittsburgh revelations came in the wake of multiple criminal investigations that focused attention on the problem since 1983, when four Kansas City Royals, including American League batting champion Willie Wilson and once-phenomenal pitcher Vida Blue, were sent to prison for cocaine use; other players were implicated but not prosecuted. After the Pittsburgh disclosures, careers came to abrupt ends, and there were suspensions and tragic endings—former relief pitcher Rod Scurry, who had pitched on three major-league teams in the 1980s, died a cocaine-related death in 1992 at age thirty-six.

But does that now mean that everything is reported? "I took a punch from Pedro Guerrero when he was playing for the Dodgers. It was an accident. I walked into a fistfight and got hit. Never got in the paper," reports Peter Schmuck, recalling his time covering baseball for the *Orange County Register.* Dan Shaughnessy, of the *Boston Globe,* spoke for many fellow beat reporters when he said on a 2001 History Channel documentary, *Baseball: Stories from the Press Box,* "If it affects the product, it's fair game."

6.2.0. There Are Unwritten Rules for Dealing with the Media

6.2.1. A Pitcher Should Never Tell the Press That He Hit a Batter Intentionally

6.2.2. A Player Should Never Admit to the Press That the Ump Made the Wrong Call on a Play That Benefited His Team

7.0.0. A Hardball Miscellany—the Unwritten Rules for Other Elements of the Game

Baseball has a number of minor unwritten rules that are not central to the game but are practiced nonetheless. These include rules for ceremonial first pitches, new ballparks, and the all-important matter of facial hair.

7.1.0. Ceremonial First Pitches: Don't Throw the Ball in the Dirt

ESPN's Tim Kurkjian, who has had considerable firsthand experience in such matters, reports: "Vice President Dick Cheney told me 'the number one rule is, never throw from the top of the mound.' As for the presidential first ball, when

President Bush threw out the first ball at the 2001 World Series at Yankee Stadium—the first World Series game after 9/11—he saw Derek Jeter before the game. He asked Jeter for advice. Jeter told him 'whatever you do, don't throw it in the dirt. This is New York, they will boo you.' Mr. Bush went to the top of the mound, and threw a strike to the plate. He got a thunderous ovation."

On March 31, 2008, at the opening of Nationals Park in Washington, President Bush again took to the mound and tossed it high—a much inferior pitch to the 2001 toss, but he kept it out of the dirt.

7.2.0. New Ballparks: Baseball Should Be Played Outside on Real Grass in a Stadium Designed Strictly for Baseball

Over time, and after seeing a group of domed and cookie-cutter stadiums built to house football as well as baseball, this unwritten rule was established, and all new stadiums should be designed with it in mind. After the advent of Camden Yards and Jacobs Field, it was clear that domes were doomed and football should find its own playgrounds.

7.3.0. All-Star Games: Managers Must Feel
Compelled to Use Everyone on Their Staff

In All-Star Games, pitchers routinely get pulled after only an inning or two of work, no matter how well they are doing, so that everyone on their staff can be used. As in all sports, there is a difference between All-Star Games and the game it is meant to showcase. There is, for example, no checking in the National Hockey League All-Star Game.

7.4.0. Uniform Numbers: Pitchers Must
Wear Double-Digit Uniform Numbers

For reasons obscured by time, uniform numbers above 39 are reserved for pitchers, except for 41, 44, and 51. The number 42, which was Jackie Robinson's, was permanently retired for all major-league and minor-league players on April 15, 1997, the fiftieth anniversary of Robinson's debut with the Dodgers.

7.5.0. Facial Hair: Management Sets Clubhouse Rules and Rules of Personal Appearance

One unwritten rule that had been in place in the major leagues for close to sixty years, from 1914 to 1972, strongly disfavored facial hair. In addition, with the growth of a counterculture in the 1960s to which hair became a virtual sacrament, several teams had instituted their own formal policies—most notably the Cincinnati Reds—forbidding team members from growing mustaches and beards.

When superstar Reggie Jackson appeared in the Oakland A's spring-training camp in Arizona in 1972, he sported a full mustache and beard, and it was clear that he intended to remain unshaven through Opening Day, when he would be the first major-league player to be documented wearing a mustache in the regular season since Wally Schang of the Philadelphia A's in 1914. Others had sported them in spring training but shaved them off for Opening Day.

Jackson's new look created a stir in the A's camp, quickly attracting the attention of A's owner Charlie Finley and manager Dick Williams. "The story as I remember it," former A's first baseman Mike Hegan told writer Bruce Markusen, who has written extensively on this moment, "was that Reggie came into spring training with a mustache, and Charlie didn't like it. So he told Dick to tell Reggie to shave it off. And Dick told Reggie to shave it off, and Reggie told Dick what to do. This got to be a real sticking point, and so I guess Charlie and Dick had a meeting, and they said, 'Reggie's an individual so maybe we can try some reverse psychology here.' Charlie told a couple of other guys to start growing a mustache. Then, [if] a couple of other guys did it, Reggie would shave his off, and you know, everything would be OK."

But Jackson would not budge. Meanwhile, Catfish Hunter—the Hall of Fame right-hander who died in 1999—grew a mustache, along with closer Rollie Fingers, who became famous for his handlebar. More players followed suit, and before long the A's were drawing media attention for their hirsute look. Sensing an easy publicity opportunity, the promotion-minded Finley offered a $300 incentive to any player who grew a mustache by Father's Day—in time for a Mustache Day promotion at Oakland-Alameda County Coliseum. By the time the A's reached the World Series against the clean-shaven Reds, so many Oakland players and coaches had mustaches or beards that the Series was dubbed the Hairs versus the Squares, and the '72 A's are still known as the Mustache Gang. Baseball's long-standing unwritten rule prohibiting facial hair has been overturned in general but held hard by some teams. The Reds did not lift their ban until 1999, when otherwise inflexible owner Marge Schott allowed Greg Vaughn to keep the goatee he sported when he arrived in a trade from the Padres.

The great irony at work here is that the 1972 A's had the collective face of one of the great teams of the nineteenth century, because the unwritten rule against facial hair replaced the exact opposite unwritten rule. Listen to Connie Mack as he reminisces in his memoir *My 66 Years in the Big Leagues*: "Ball players in the early days thought it was a sign of manhood to raise a beard. You couldn't be an athlete without raising whiskers or at least a mustache. In fact, most of the players on the Washington Senators, when I was a catcher back in 1887, wore mustaches."

Today, there are some clubs that allow facial hair and some that ban it outright. When Joe Girardi took over the Yankees in the spring of 2008, he replaced Joe Torre's long-standing rule of no facial hair with a new standard permitting neatly cut beards, mustaches, and goatees. No long hair or "unshaven looks" are allowed, however.

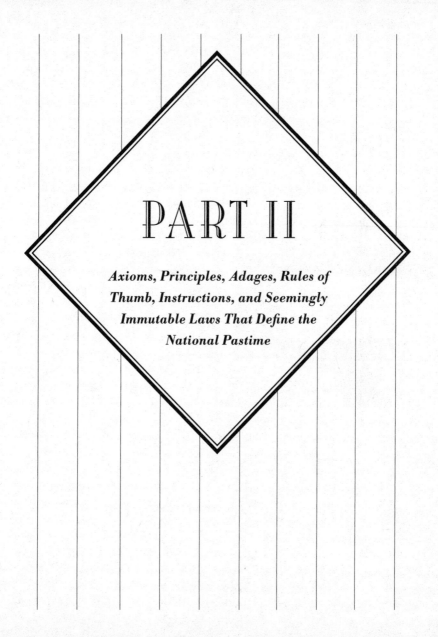

PART II

Axioms, Principles, Adages, Rules of Thumb, Instructions, and Seemingly Immutable Laws That Define the National Pastime

How many times have you read or heard something like "an old baseball axiom suggests that," or "tonight an old baseball adage rings true"? There are scores of these pithy axioms, adages, and aphorisms, ranging from blatant truisms—"You can't win 'em all"—to questionable barstool assertions—"Pitching is 75 percent of baseball" (or "80 percent" or "90 percent" or whatever number sounds good to you). Then there are those that once ruled but now no longer do—for most of the twentieth century, the axiom in the Northeast was "As the temperature drops, so do the Red Sox."

These are all part of a larger body of conventional wisdom—aphorisms, laws, principles, and lists of instruction—that seem to be peculiar to the game of baseball and begin with the ritual of buying a program or scorecard, because even in the age of the jumbo electronic scoreboard, fans still repeat the old baseball adage "You can't tell the players without a scorecard."

It is as if those associated with the game are always attempting to create an orderly universe out of the game in which the keys to success and failure can be reduced to a series of pithy mock-scientific observations. They are heard in dugouts, broadcast booths, and press boxes; are repeated by fans; and are increasingly fodder for the ever-proliferating population of baseball Web pages and blogs.

I have been collecting baseball axioms such as these for many years and present them here in one place listed by topic or under the person's name, as relevant. Taken together, they represent a collective conventional wisdom that has attached itself to the game.

As often as not, these truisms and hypotheses find their way into other sports and other walks of life. One's first tennis lesson is likely to include a quote from "Wee Willie" Keeler about hitting them where they ain't, and those unwilling to take risks in business are reminded that you can't steal second with one foot on first base.

A warning here is that like nonbaseball "truisms," these are often contradictory. So be it. This is known as the "first law of the axiom," which holds that for every axiom there is an equal and opposite axiom. To make money in baseball, you need a team in contention, and to have a team in contention, you have to spend money—a saying that gained ground with the teams of Connie Mack, who had paid more than $100,000 to sign Lefty Grove in the mid-1920s. But then we are told you cannot buy a contender. We are told that "winners breed winners," but also that that one of the most difficult things to do in baseball is repeat.

Age. Most players peak between the ages of twenty-seven and thirty-two. —This axiom was temporarily suspended during the Steroid Era.

Alston's Truest Axiom. "Perhaps the truest axiom in baseball is that the toughest thing to do is repeat. The tendency is to relax without even knowing it, the feeling being, 'we did it last year, so we can do it again.'" —Walter Alston, as manager of the Los Angeles Dodgers, quoted in the *Los Angeles Herald-Examiner,* February 27, 1975.

Andujar's Constant. "There is one word in America that says it all, and that one word is, 'youneverknow.'" —Dominican pitcher and Cardinals great Joaquin Andujar, quoted first in *Sports Illustrated*, June 22, 1987. Andujar *never allowed a grand slam home run, but he did hit one.* "Youneverknow." The term applies to other baseball axioms and aphorisms, such as "You never know a guy until you have him on your club."

Angell's Aphorism. "Baseball is simple but never easy." —*New Yorker* baseball writer Roger Angell in *Late Innings: A Baseball Companion* (1982).

Annie Savoy's Credo. "I believe in the Church of Baseball. I've tried all the major religions, and most of the minor ones. I've worshipped Buddha, Allah, Brahma, Vishnu, Siva, trees, mushrooms, and Isadora Duncan. I know things. For instance, there are 108 beads in a Catholic rosary and there are 108 stitches in a baseball. When I heard that, I gave Jesus a chance. But it just didn't work out between us. The Lord laid too much guilt on me. I prefer metaphysics to theology. You see, there's no guilt in baseball . . . I've tried 'em all, I really have, and the only church that truly feeds the soul, day in, day out, is the Church of Baseball." —The character Annie Savoy in the film *Bull Durham* (1988).

The Any-Given-Team Paradox. You are never as good as you look when you're winning or as bad as you look when you're losing. —The wisdom in that statement is undeniable, in that the differences between teams on a tear and those in free fall are often temporary and sometimes minor. Every team looks hopeless when they are playing badly. The Dodgers lost sixteen of twenty-two in early 2004 and seemed headed for the cellar. Then there was the 22–0 drubbing of the New York Yankees by the Indians on August 31 of the same year.

The Anything-Can-Happen Axiom. Anything can happen in baseball. —Back in 1962, while watching pitcher Gaylord Perry in batting practice, Alvin Dark, then manager of the San Francisco Giants, said, "There will be a man on the moon before he hits a home run in the big leagues." Seven years later, thirty-four minutes after *Apollo 11* landed on the moon, Perry hit his first major-league home run.

April. (1) You can't win a pennant in April, but you can lose one. (2) Rookies who bloom in the spring, tra la, are often back in the minor leagues by May 1.

Automotive Adage. Singles hitters don't drive Cadillacs. —From an earlier time when salaries were a fraction of those paid today and Cadillacs were the most sought after luxury cars.

Avery's Saying. "No ball game is ever much good unless the people involved hate each other." —H. Allen Smith, from *Let the Crabgrass Grow* (1960). Avery was Smith's aphoristic and fictional neighbor whose utterings also included "There is no such thing as too much point on a pencil" and "When there are two conflicting versions of a story, the wise course is to believe the one in which people appear at their worst."

"Babe Ruth Is . . ." (1) ". . . dead, so throw fastballs." (2) ". . . dead and buried in Baltimore, but the game is bigger and better than ever." —Quotes by Sparky Anderson while manager of the Detroit Tigers. Ruth is actually buried in Gate of Heaven Cemetery in Westchester County, New York.

Baker's Rule of Journalism. "Every general interest newspaper columnist is required to write one column a year waxing poetic about baseball." —Russell Baker of the *New York Times* in an April 7, 1992, column objecting to the requirement.

Banks's Dictum. "It's a great day for a ball game. Let's play two!" —The Chicago Cubs' Ernie Banks's most famous line and one of the reasons he attracted the honorific title of "Mr. Baseball." The line is quoted often and widely and tends to be uttered when the weather is mild and the players are primed.

Barry's Razor. "If a woman has to choose between catching a fly ball and saving an infant's life, she will save the infant's life without even considering if there are men on base." — Dave Barry, from his syndicated column of March 10, 1985.

The Baseball Principle. "You can't help the Mets by watching them on TV." —Articulated and explored by N. David Mermin, a physicist with a philosophical bent and a passion for baseball. At Cornell University in Ithaca, New York, Mermin uses this concept to illustrate a point in the realm of quantum mechanics. He asserts that true baseball fans feel deep inside that their watching a game on TV really does influence the game. But, forced to be rational, most fans realize that whether they watch a game on TV has no effect on the game's outcome. "What I do or don't do in Ithaca, N.Y., will have no effect on what the Mets do or don't do in Flushing, N.Y.," Mermin says. "I call this the Baseball Principle. You can't help the Mets by watching them on TV." Quoted by Ivars Peterson, "Quantum Baseball: A Baseball Analogy Illuminates A Paradox of Quantum Mechanics," *Science News*, August 5, 1989.

Baseball's Laws of Averages. (1) No team shall completely dominate another. (2) Everything evens out in the end. —For every hard-hit out there's a bloop single. For every 1–0 loss a pitcher endures, there's a victory he earns that he doesn't deserve. Another version of this is that breaks even out over the long haul.

Baseball's Own Rules of Analysis: The Known Principles of Sabermetrics. (1) There are two essential elements of an offense: its ability to get people on base and its ability to advance runners. (2) Batting and pitching statistics never represent pure accomplishments, but are heavily colored by all kinds of illusions and extraneous effects. One of the most important of these is park effects. (3) There is a predictable relationship between the number of runs a team scores, the number it allows, and the number of games that it will win.

Batting Averages. (1) It's harder to maintain your batting average when it's high to begin with. (2) In order to make the major leagues, a player must be able to hit his own weight. (3) Over time, the league averages are about .265. —The parity between hitting and pitching is maintained perfectly at this point, and has been so for decades. *Corollary*: Because of this equilibrium, there will never be another .400 hitter.

Batting Coaches. Great hitters make poor hitting coaches. —Axiom invoked with Ted Williams as the prime example—the man who could hit .400 but could not teach batting himself. The modern exception to the rule seems to be Yankees hitting coach Don Mattingly, who spent three seasons (2004–2006) in that role, receiving much praise from the Yankees organization and his players.

Batting Slumps. Players who are in a batting slump often fall off in their fielding as well.

Beane's Law of Attrition. "Baseball is a game of attrition. Force the starting pitcher to throw as many pitches as possible, then get the less talented relievers into the game." —Billy Beane, former Major League Baseball player and the current general manager of the Oakland Athletics.

The Bench. (1) Your club is only as good as your bench. (2) "The strength of a modern major league team lies in its substitutes." —Observation made originally in 1907 by writer I. E. Sanborn.

Berra's Clarification. "It's déjà vu all over again." —Yogi Berra, widely quoted.

Blowouts. Save some runs for tomorrow. —A rallying cry that a team not waste too many runs on the winning end of a blowout, since it's a single game and hitters may be too tired to get runs in for the next game, resulting in a loss.

Boswell's Big Bang Theory. In a majority of games, the winning team scores as many or more runs in one inning than the losing team scores in the whole game; the notion that baseball is a game of *big innings*. —The name was given to the theory by *Washington Post* baseball writer Thomas Boswell (*How Life Imitates the World Series,* 1982), and given impetus by Earl Weaver's hypothesis that pitching, defense, and three-run home runs win baseball games. Research by David W. Smith (*By the Numbers,* June 1992) has suggested that big bangs generally occur when the losing team scores only one or two runs and are, therefore, more a function of good pitching than of big innings.

Bowa's Chemical Formulae. "Winning creates chemistry, and losing means bad chemistry. How can you have good chemistry if you are losing? If you're losing, you shouldn't be happy, and if you are happy when you're losing then you need to get another occupation." —Larry Bowa, manager of the Philadelphia Phillies, quoted in the *Houston Chronicle,* July 7, 2002.

Box Score Gospel. "[A] baseball box score is a democratic thing. It doesn't tell how big you are, what church you attend, what color you are, or how your father voted in the last election. It just tells what kind of baseball player you were on that particular day." —Said to Jackie Robinson; quoted in Robinson's *I Never Had It Made* (New York: G. P. Putnam's Sons, 1972).

Brabender's Law. "The most inactive player during the World Series will be the most active during the clubhouse follies." —Named for Gene Brabender of the Baltimore Orioles, who first demonstrated the law in the 1966 World Series. The law was named by George Vecsey of the *New York Times,* who noted that Brabender never got off the bullpen bench during the four-game sweep of the Los Angeles Dodgers but "went nuts" spraying fellow players, writers, and innocent bystanders with champagne.

Brosnan's Rediscovery of a Hoary Baseball Maxim. "Buy a home in the town in which you play, and you'll be traded away before your first lawn blows away." —Jim Brosnan, in *The Long Season,* on buying a house near Chicago after two years with the Cubs, only to be traded to St. Louis six months later.

C

Carmen's List of Responses to Reporters.

1. I'm just glad to be here. I just want to help the club any way I can.
2. Baseball's a funny game.
3. I'd rather be lucky than good.
4. We're going to take the season one game at a time.
5. You're only as good as your last game (last at bat).
6. This game has really changed.
7. If we stay healthy we should be right there.
8. It takes 24 (25) players.
9. We need two more players to take us over the top: Babe Ruth and Lou Gehrig.
10. We have a different hero every day.
11. We'll get 'em tomorrow.
12. This team seems ready to get hot.
13. With a couple breaks, we win that game.
14. That All-Star voting is a joke.
15. The catcher and I were on the same wavelength.

16. I just went right at 'em.

17. I did my best and that's all I can do.

18. You just can't pitch behind.

19. That's the name of the game.

20. We've got to have fun.

21. I didn't have my good stuff, but I battled 'em.

22. Give the guy some credit; he hit a good pitch.

23. Hey, we were due to catch a break or two.

24. Yes.

25. No.

26. That's why they pay him ____ million dollars.

27. Even I could have hit that pitch.

28. I know you are, but what am I?

29. I was getting my off-speed stuff over so they couldn't sit on the fastball.

30. I have my at 'em ball going today.

31. I had some great plays made behind me tonight.

32. I couldn't have done it without my teammates.

33. You saw it . . . write it.

34. I just wanted to go as hard as I could as long as I could.

35. I'm seeing the ball real good.

36. I hit that ball good.

37. I don't get paid to hit.

—Philly reliever Don Carmen had these clichés posted on his locker during the 1990 season. They were offered to reporters with the line "You saw the game, take what you need." They appeared in an Associated Press item on June 23, 1990.

Caribbean Baseball. "You can't get off an island by walking." —Julio Franco, born in the Dominican Republic, who helped establish the idea that the players who want to move from the Caribbean islands to the major leagues can get there only through aggressive ballplaying and not taking walks. "If you don't swing, you can't get a hit," Raul Mondesi said in 1994 and quoted in *Sports Illustrated* on May 30. "I'm just a rookie, and I'm trying as hard as I can. After five or six years maybe I'll take some pitches."

Carter's Conclusion. "They don't put spring-training statistics on the back of bubble-gum cards." —Blue Jays slugger Joe Carter on getting just one extra-base hit in fifty-nine spring training at bats, as reported in the *St. Louis Post-Dispatch*, April 21, 1993.

Catchers. (1) Catchers are always in short supply. (2) The fastest way to the majors is as a catcher. *Corollary:* A switch-hitting catcher with a strong arm tends to move to the majors even faster. (3) A catcher never lets anyone mess with his pitcher.

Caudill's Law on Losing. "Even Betty Crocker burns a cake now and then." —Bill Caudill, Oakland A's, 1984. Posted on the wall of the Home Plate Diner in Lubbock, Texas (from Tom Gill).

Cellar Dwellers. Coming down the stretch, tail-end clubs can be treacherous because they are totally relaxed.

Central Baseball Truism. You win some, you lose some, and some are rained out. —This traditional truism has been applied widely outside of baseball and given added life when uttered by Nuke LaLoosh in the film *Bull Durham.*

Cerebral Caution. Thinking is stinking. —The reasoning here is that when you start thinking, "How much pressure should I put into my throw? Should I try to reach first base a certain way?" you are gone. In the 1988 film *Bull Durham,* Crash Davis, the Durham Bulls' new catcher, is advised by his manager to mentor Nuke LaLoosh, a flame-throwing pitcher with control issues, both in life and on the mound. "Don't think," Crash tells Nuke. "It can only hurt the ball club."

Cinema Verité. (1) Movies about baseball tend to be better than movies about other sports, except for boxing. (2) One can have only one good baseball movie per acting career. *Corollary*: This assumes that one believes that Kevin Costner should have quit while ahead (e.g., *Bull Durham* versus *Field of Dreams* and *For Love of the Game*).

Clubhouse Admonitions. (1) What happens out there is influenced by what happens in here. (2) NO GAMBLING. (3) YOU CAN'T MAKE THE CLUB IN THE TUB. —In *Baseball Is a Funny Game*, Joe Garagiola writes, "Ever wonder if somebody painted 'fighting phrases' on the walls of a clubhouse? In baseball that is rare," adding that the only sign he had ever seen on a clubhouse wall was the admonition to eschew excessive bathing, which was on the wall in Pittsburgh.

Cobb's Keys to Baseball Success. (1) Learn the fundamentals. (2) Study and work at the game as if it were a science. (3) Keep in top physical condition. (4) Make yourself as effective as possible. (5) Get the desire to win. (6) Keeping in the best physical condition and having an intense spirit to succeed is the combination for winning games. —Ty Cobb's "Six Keys to Baseball Success," quoted in *Sporting News*, February 20, 1957.

Constants. (1) Hitting and defense may come and go on a game-by-game basis. But speed never takes a day off. It's always there. (2) Those bases on balls will kill you every time.

Cook's Truism. "A lot of bad stuff happens when your starting pitcher can't get past the fifth inning game after game." —Ron Cook in the *Pittsburgh Post-Gazette,* April 14, 2006.

The Count. If you run counts, you count runs. —If a batter takes a pitcher deep into the count, he will often make him more predictable, improve his own timing, and, thus, be more likely to get a hit. Tony Gwynn was a master at working the count. From the pitcher's standpoint, the best pitch is a first-pitch strike, which makes it much easier to stay ahead in the count.

Curveball Truism. Good hitting is no match for the subtle power of a huge, left-handed curveball.

Custodiet's Complement. The human hand is made complete by the addition of a baseball. —Unknown origin, from aphorism collector Ryan Anthony, and first published in *The Official Explanations* (1980). The name that has been attached to this assertion is elusive. *Custodiet* is a Latin verb meaning "to watch" or "to guard" and appears in a well-known quote from Juvenal, *"Quis custodiet ipsos custodes,"* which roughly translated means "Who will watch the watchmen" or "Who will guard the guards." It was invoked during the Steroid Era in baseball.

Davis's Distinction. "Strikeouts are fascist. Ground balls are democratic." —The character Crash Davis in the 1988 film *Bull Durham*.

Defense. (1) No club is ever successful unless it is strong through the middle. (2) The shortstop is considered the "middle of the middle." (3) It is difficult to win with youth up the middle. *Corollary:* Especially when they give you little offensive power. (4) If your team cannot field a ground ball or catch a pop fly, it doesn't much matter who you have pitching or hitting. (5) The ball will find anybody sent on the field as a desperate stopgap measure. (6) A player who makes a good defensive play to end an inning is often the next to bat. (7) A player who makes a good defensive play often follows that up in the next inning with an offensive play. —In its April 5, 2004, issue, *Sports Illustrated* carried an article by Roy Blount Jr. claiming the seventh axiom is demonstrably wrong, citing the work of a professor named "Yorik," as in the Shakespearean quote "Alas, poor Yorick! . . . a fellow of infinite jest." Yorik devised a formula called "Lead

Off/Outstanding Fielding Alignment," or LOOFA, to debunk the baseball myth. It is, of course, an April Fool's Day piece—LOOFA spelled backward is "a fool," and there are so many clues to this fact that they overwhelm Juan Abril (pronounced "One Abril"). "Abril" is an authority cited in the piece, and the story mentioned the '41 Society, an "informal association of baseball buffs" who criticize the report. 4–1 is the numerical form of April 1, and the story claims that the LOOFA phenomenon happened 40.1 percent of the time in one era, 41 percent another, and .041 percent in the last thirteen years. Again, all the numbers are a numerical form for April 1. The theme of the magazine's baseball preview issue is the growing trend for baseball teams to rely on statistics to make decisions about personnel and game strategy. The Blount story seemingly uses statistics to poke holes in one of baseball's oldest mythological coincidences—that of a player batting right after making a great defensive play.

The Devil. "For the afternoon had proved an axiom long known to baseball men, and known now even to Applegate. And this was that not even the devil could force an umpire to change his decision." —Lesson learned by the devil in the person of Applegate in *The Year the Yankees*

Lost the Pennant, by Douglass Wallop (1954). The line "not even the devil could force an umpire to change his decision," became famous when the book was transformed into *Damn Yankees* on Broadway and in Hollywood.

DiMaggio's Distinction. "No outfielder is a real workman unless he can turn his back on the ball, run his legs off and make the catch over his shoulder. Practice this play until you are sure of it. Backpedaling outfielders get nowhere." —Joe DiMaggio, from his *Baseball for Everyone* (New York: Whittlesey House, 1948).

Don'ts. (1) Don't try to get it all back with one swing. (2) Don't mess with a player's superstitions. (3) Don't believe what you see in April and September (that is, don't believe what you see of fast starts in April or fast finishes in September by an out-of-the-race team).

Doubleheaders. It's hard to win a doubleheader and easy to lose one.

Drysdale's Plunk Ratio. "For every one of ours you hit, I'll hit two of yours." —Don Drysdale of the 1956–1969 Dodgers. Drysdale used brushback pitches and a sidearm fastball to intimidate batters. His record 154 hit batsmen remains a modern National League record.

Dugan's Baseball Prayer. "Uh, Lord, hallowed be Thy name. May our feet be swift; may our bats be mighty; may our balls . . . be plentiful. Lord, I'd just like to thank You for that waitress in South Bend. You know who she is—she kept calling Your name. And God, these are good girls, and they work hard. Just help them see it all the way through. Okay, that's it." —The character Jimmy Dugan, played by Tom Hanks, in the film *A League of Their Own* (1992).

Duracell Rule. "If there is a close play in right field at Yankee Stadium, never, ever rule against the home team for fear of getting a concussion from a shower of batteries." —Thom Loverro, *Washington Times,* October 10, 1996.

Dykes's Rule. "The manager's toughest job is not calling the right play with the bases full and the score tied in an extra inning game. It's telling a player that he's through, done, finished." —Former player Jimmy Dykes, longtime manager of the Chicago White Sox (from 1934 to 1946). From his autobiography *You Can't Steal First Base* (1967), which is also the source of the following entry.

Dykes's Truisms. Speed's great, but you can't steal first base. —Batters with low on-base percentages are not able to rack up many steals. The best leadoff men have one thing in common—the ability to reach base about 40 percent of the time.

E

Equation. Walk = single. —A saying that suggests a walk is just as good as a single, in that a player gets on first base by either method. Even though a hitter won't drive in base runners with a walk, unless the bases are loaded, it still keeps a rally going.

Eskenazi's Rule for Rookie Baseball Writers. "Always get the score in the first paragraph." —Gerald Eskenazi, reflecting on his first baseball assignment at the *New York Times* as recalled in *A Sportswriter's Life* (2004). "Imagine . . . that in the body of every baseball story we wrote in the fifties and sixties we even had to mention the name of the team's manager and what league the team was in."

F

The Fastball. No matter how fast a fastball travels, someone, somehow, will catch up to it.

The Flake Rule. The more screws you've got loose, the more you're one of the guys.

Foley's Opening Day Rule for Politicians. "Don't throw a baseball unless you have a very high box to drop it from . . . straight down. Do not go out on the mound and try to toss it across the field." —Former House Speaker Tom Foley to a group of reporters on June 22, 1992, reacting to Dan Quayle's problem in spelling *potato(e)* at a spelling bee.

Formulae for Winning Seasons. (1) If a team beats up on the weaklings and breaks even with the contenders, it's going to be all right. (2) Most teams are sure to win sixty games and lose sixty games in a season. What happens in the other forty-two separates the champions from the also-rans. Within those forty-two are a half dozen that defy logic. Nobody really can explain the hows and whys of the final number of wins and losses.

Fourth of July. The team in first place on July 4 will win the division. —Like most axioms, no one is exactly sure where this one came from, but it had become so strongly entrenched that in 1928 the Negro American League, a southern league that included the Atlanta Black Crackers and the Memphis Red Sox, had a split season to allow for two championships. The idea was abandoned because it seemed to have a negative impact on attendance, but as late as 1930 there was still talk in the league of reviving the idea. But, according to Jay Jaffe of the *New York Sun,* a 1934 *Time* magazine cover story noted that in the previous twenty-five years, the leader on July 4 had gone on to the World Series two-thirds of the time. Since then, the major leagues have expanded from sixteen to thirty teams, adding two pre-liminary play-off rounds while quadrupling the number of clubs invited to the postseason. But, based on Jaffe's research, the predictive power of Independence Day remains intact—about two-thirds in the one-division era (62.7 percent) as well as the three-division era (63.5 percent). Articulated by Henry Schulman of the *San Francisco Chronicle* in 2002.

Freehan's Laws. (1) Never beat yourself. (2) Always play an expansion club or very weak team toward the end of July and through August, if possible. —Catcher Bill Freehan, from his finely focused memoir of the 1969 season, *Behind the Mask* (1970).

Frick's Ten Commandments of Umpiring.

   1. Keep your eye on the ball.

2. Keep all your personalities out of your work. Forget and forgive.

3. Avoid sarcasm. Don't insist on the last word.

4. Never charge a player and, above all, no pointing your finger or yelling.

5. Hear only the things you should hear—be deaf to others.

6. Keep your temper. A decision made in anger is never sound.

7. Watch your language.

8. Take pride in your work at all times. Remember, respect for an umpire is created off the field as well as on.

9. Review your work. You will find, if you are honest, that 90% of the trouble is traceable to loafing.

10. No matter what your opinion of another umpire, never make an adverse comment regarding him. To do so is despicable and ungentlemanly.

—Ford C. Frick, as commissioner of Major League Baseball, who created them in 1949. They were published in the June 1949 issue of *Baseball Digest,* which added editorially that persons other than umpires might accept and put into practice some of Frick's suggestions.

Garagiola's Warning. "Never trust a base runner who's limping. Comes a base hit and you'll think he just got back from Lourdes." —Joe Garagiola, from *Baseball Is a Funny Game* (1960).

Geffner's Caution. "Don't count on baby hurlers before they hatch." — Michael P. Geffner, "Metropolitan Meltdown," *Sporting News*, August 19, 1996.

The Axiom of the Glove. The harder a ball goes in, the harder it seems to come back out.

Golden Rule of the Diamond. Do unto others as they do unto you. And do it in the early innings.

Golf/Baseball Maxims and Distinctions. (1) **Aaron's Calculation.** "It took me seventeen years to get 3,000 hits in baseball. I did it in one afternoon on the golf course." —Baseball Hall of Famer Hank Aaron, quoted in the *Orlando Sentinel*, June 16, 1985. (2) **Snead's Distinction.** "When we hit a foul ball, we've gotta get out there and play it." —"Slamming Sammy" Snead to Ted Williams, who, along with his Red Sox teammates, were ribbing Snead about golf's inferiority to baseball. Reported in *Time*, June 21, 1954. See also *Plimpton's Correlation.*

Gomez's Law. If you don't throw it, they can't hit it. —Lefty Gomez.

Gomez's Prescription for a Successful Pitching Career. Clean living and a fast outfield. —Lefty Gomez, who led both leagues for many years in self-deprecation, saying, for example, "I was the worst hitter ever. I never even broke a bat until last year when I was backing out of the garage."

Green's Motto. THE WILL TO WIN IS NOT WORTH A NICKEL UNLESS YOU HAVE THE WILL TO PRACTICE. —Dallas Green, posted on clubhouse wall when he managed the Yankees in 1989. Such mottos were spread throughout various clubhouses ruled by Green. Another: A GREAT PLEASURE IN LIFE IS DOING WHAT PEOPLE SAY YOU CANNOT DO.

Griffey's Advice for Defending against Barry Bonds. "Stick the infielders in the outfield and stick the outfielders in the seats." —Ken Griffey, quoted in the *Cleveland Plain Dealer*, May 16, 2004.

H

Rickey Henderson's Rules for a Long Career. (1) Run three to five miles every other day. "Some guys, once the season starts, they relax, eat, do nothing. I feel sluggish that way. I got to get up and do something, get the blood back circulating and get the oxygen back in my body." (2) Do two hundred sit-ups and one hundred push-ups a day. "I don't do a lot of weights. Some guys, they want to be Hulk Hogan. Not me." (3) Stretch before bedtime. "Do your stretching before you sleep. That way you wake up loose." (4) Eat plenty of ice cream. "I like to eat ice cream at night. I got to have something sweet before I go to sleep." —Quoted by Tom Verducci in *Sports Illustrated,* June 23, 2003.

Highs and Lows. Keep your highs low and your lows high. —An axiom with special relevance in the minor leagues. "It's a tough thing to learn," Paul Rappoli, a former minor leaguer who trains young players in the Boston area, told the *Boston Globe.* "You go 4-for-4 and you're sky high. You think you are ready for the majors. Then, the next day you strike out four times and you feel like quitting the game. You can't do that. You have to be able to bounce back from adversity. That's what the scouts really look for." Quoted by Paul Harber, "Chasing the Dream of Playing Big-League Ball—Veterans Offer Survival Guide for Local Players," *Boston Globe*, June 29, 2003.

Hitters. (1) Up at bat, you are totally alone. (2) Hitters murder fastballs. —"But nobody murders a 100-m.p.h. fastball," wrote Pat Jordan in the *New York Times Magazine* in an article on the fastest of fastballs entitled "The Hardest Stuff." The difference between a 97 mph fastball and a 100 mph fastball, Jeff Bagwell told Jordan, "is that sometimes you don't see it until it's in your face. It's a macho confrontation. You can see it in a pitcher's eyes—he wants to dominate you. I like that." Jordan pointed out that a 100 mph fastball reaches the catcher four-tenths of a second after it leaves the pitcher's hand. A batter has fifteen-hundredths of a second to react to a 100 mph fastball.

Hitting. (1) A team that does not hit does not win. (2) Hitting is contagious. (3) Not hitting is contagious. (4). If you can hit, they'll find a spot for you. (5) Anybody with a bat in his hands can be dangerous—even a pitcher with a hitless past. (There are a number of examples of this fifth axiom at work but few as direct as Greg Hibbard's first major-league hit for the Cubs on August 8, 1993, when he drove in the winning run to beat the Cardinals 2–1.

He was 0-for-35 at the plate with no RBIs [runs batted in] for the season before hitting the double.) (6) Poor hitting beats poor pitching.

Home Field. (1) If you play .700 at home and .500 on the road, you have a chance to win. *Corollary:* Anything over .500 on the road is a bonus. (2) Over the course of a season, home-field superiority will assert itself.

Home Runs. (1) Home runs are nice, but they aren't always everything. (Often, teams leading their leagues in home runs late in the season are not going to make the playoffs.) (2) Solo homers are rally killers.

Hubbell's Ten Commandments for Pitching Aspirants.
1. A limber arm.
2. A rugged physique, or, as an alternative, wiriness.
3. A repertoire, meaning a fastball and at least one breaking ball, preferably a curve.
4. Control.
5. Competitive courage.
6. Endurance.
7. Intelligence.
8. The ability to size up a hitter.
9. Confidence.
10. Fielding skill.

—Carl Hubbell, quoted in *The Official Encyclopedia of Baseball* (1956), condensed from the book *Playing the Giants Game* (New York: National Exhibition Co., 1949).

Hurst's Benediction. "The pay is good, it keeps you out in the fresh air and sunshine, and you can't beat the hours."

—Umpire Tim Hurst, on the benefits of big-league baseball, first quoted by Jim Brosnan in the *New York Times*, April 7, 1966. Hurst's career as an umpire ended in 1909 when he spit in the eye of the Philadelphia Athletics' second baseman, igniting a riot.

I

The Ten Commandments of the Idiot Fan.
1. Thou shall use batting average and RBIs to measure a player's worth.
2. Thou shall respect owners as courageous captains of industry.
3. Thou shall attribute a player's failure to moral weakness.
4. Thou shall believe the bunt is a viable offensive weapon to be used in any inning.

5. Thou shall believe that a player who draws a walk is afraid to try to get a hit.

6. Thou shall pass judgment on a player's effort by the amount of dirt on his uniform.

7. Thou shall treat the seventh-inning stretch with reverence.

8. Thou shall drone incessantly about the virtues of clutch hitting.

9. Thou shall always blame players' salaries for the high price of tickets and concessions. *Corollary*: Thou shall never use the word *agent* without the word *greedy* in front of it.

10. Thou shall believe that small-market teams cannot win.

—These rules were posted on an AOL site for hard-core fans on December 10, 2004, and were immediately embellished by characterizations of the idiot fan. One commenter offered a description of the ideal Idiot Fan: "Bottom of the eighth, and your team is finally starting to make some noise with the tying run in the on-deck circle. The guy in the front row of your section who so far has paid no attention to anyone other than his buddies and the beer guy, notices something is going on on the field. He stands up, turns around, lifts his arms up and starts telling everyone behind him to get up and scream." That guy is an example of the Idiot Fan. They have only one commandment: Thou shall be as obnoxious as possible without any trace of humor.

Immutable Law of the Departed. "The worse a player performs for you, the better he'll play against you after he's gone." —So stated by Andrew Baggarly in *Inside Bay Area,* May 27, 2005, who wrote on this law. "Ricky Ledee stepped neatly into his moment in time Thursday night. A miserable failure as a late-season pickup with the Giants last season, Ledee grounded a two-run single off Tyler Walker to snap a tie in the ninth inning as the Dodgers won 6–4 at SBC Park to avoid a three-game sweep."

Imponderable. The player on the field who records the last out of an inning must look over the ball several times before tossing it to the umpire.

Injury Axiom. "If a team's talent is not deep enough to overcome a rash of injuries to its starters, the team will not win." —Stated by Murray Chass in the *New York Times,* May 28, 1995, as an "old baseball axiom." He used it to predict that the injury-plagued Yankees would not win the American League East. They came in second and were eliminated in the play-offs by the Mariners.

It Ain't Over . . . (1) till it's over. (2) until the first Cub comes

to bat. —Dizzy Dean to a St. Louis Cardinals broadcaster, reported by Arch Ward in the *Chicago Tribune,*
July 7, 1949.

It's Nots. (1) It's not how, it's how many. (2) It's not who has
the better team, it's who plays the better ball.

Jackson's Imperative. "Baseball players must spit when the
television camera closes in on them." —Michael Jackson,
a radio host for three decades at KABC, Los Angeles.

James's Axioms. (1) A ballplayer's purpose in playing ball is
to do those things that create wins for his team, while
avoiding those things that create losses for his team. (2)
Wins result from runs scored. Losses result from runs
allowed. *Corollary:* An offensive player's job is to create
runs for his team. (3) All offense and all defense occurs
within a context of outs. —The heart of Bill James's sta-
tistical analysis.

James's Distinction. "Intelligent" is a term used for someone
who agrees with you. "Brilliant" means that you agree

with him, but would never have thought of the idea yourself. —Baseball writer and analyst Bill James, in his *1983 Baseball Abstract*.

Jinxes. The greatest jinx is the spoken word.

The Jordan Principle. "Genius doesn't travel well." —Created by Robert J. Samuelson in the *Washington Post,* March 5, 1997, and named in honor of Michael Jordan's attempt to break into baseball with the AA Birmingham Barons. It has wide application—just because you made a lot of money does not make you an economic philosopher.

$$\text{K}$$

Keeler's Constants. (1) Keep your eye clear. (2) Keep your temper cool. (3) Hit 'em where they ain't. —William H. "Wee Willie" Keeler (1872–1923), one of the greatest batsmen of all time, not as a slugger but as a place hitter.

Koppett's Distinction. "A thrower gets people out because he has so much stuff on the ball that players just can't hit it. A pitcher makes full use of the art of keeping hitters off balance, with or without hard stuff." —The late

Leonard Koppett, from *The Thinking Fan's Guide to Baseball* (1966).

Koppett's Rule. "Baseball will inconvenience the largest number of people as often as possible." —Leonard Koppett, quoted widely at the time of his death at age seventy-nine (June 22, 2003) by Hal Bodley in *USA Today*, June 24, 2003. Bodley stated that for many years the first thing that a rookie baseball writer learned was this rule. "During long rain delays, inconvenient schedule changes, day-long waits for owners' meetings to end, tired reporters would grouse 'Remember Koppett's Rule.'"

Kuenn's Constant. "There's no defense for the home run unless you buy a seat in the bleachers." —Harvey Kuenn, as manager of the Milwaukee Brewers, quoted in the *Wisconsin State Journal*, August, 12, 2007.

L

Labor Day Razor. The general rule of thumb in baseball is that a club eliminated from the pennant race before Labor Day has had a very bad year.

La Russa's Managerial Tenet. "When I first became a manager, I asked Chuck Tanner for advice. He told me, 'Always rent.'" —Tony La Russa, quoted in Bill Adler's *Baseball Wit* (1986).

Lasorda's Advisory. "You don't want to have a knuckleballer pitching for you or against you." —Tommy Lasorda on first seeing Phil Niekro pitch, quoted by Hal Bock of the Associated Press on Niekro's induction into the Hall of Fame in 1997.

Lau's Conclusion. There are two theories on hitting the knuckleball. Unfortunately, neither of them work. —The late Charley Lau Sr., a legendary batting coach, and embellished by his son, Charley Lau Jr., whose own reputation rose rapidly when Seattle Mariners shortstop Alex Rodriguez, who hit .232 in 1995, used Lau's system to hit .358 and win the American League batting title during the 1996 season. Since then, Lau has worked with other high-profile players, including Tony Gwynn, Dante Bichette, and many more.

Lau's Five Most Common Flaws in the Swing. (1) Bad stance, unorthodox launch position. (2) Starting too late. (3) Staying on the back side too long. (4) Trying to muscle the ball. (5) Top-hand rollover. —The late Charley Lau Sr., from *Charley Lau's Laws on Hitting*.

Lau's Laws on Hitting. (1) Use a balanced and workable stance. (2) Use a proper grip. (3) Get your weight back before striding. (4) Start your bat in the launch position. (5) Stride with your front toe closed. (6) Maintain flat hands through the swing. (7) Keep your head still and eyes down. (8) Use a fluid, tension-free swing. (9) You must have lead-arm extension and a good finish. (10) Employ solid practice habits. —The late Charley Lau Sr., quoted widely, and most recently, in *Charley Lau's Laws on Hitting* (2000).

Law's Law. "There is one place where pennants are won and lost, and that is the bullpen." —Vernon Law, as a starter for the Pittsburgh Pirates, quoted in the *Chicago Tribune*, August 19, 1966.

The Left-Handed. (1) Left-handers take longer to develop. (Articulated by Andy MacPhail and others.) (2) Left-handers are not supposed to throw change-ups to left-handed hitters.

Line of Defense. The team with the best fielders on a line from home plate to center field (catcher, shortstop, second baseman, and center fielder) will always be a contender. —The rationale for this is simply that the catcher runs the game, the shortstop controls the infield, and the center fielder quarterbacks the outfield.

Little League Ten Commandments for Parents.

1. I shall not criticize the umpire unless ready to assume his duties.

2. I shall not complain about anyone unless I have labored more hours on Little League programs than they have.

3. I shall not be a grandstand manager.

4. I shall remember that only nine team members can play at any one time.

5. I shall set an example of sportsmanship for my child to follow.

6. I shall not be critical unless willing to put out the necessary effort to correct my criticism.

7. I shall remember that all managers, coaches, team moms, officers, directors and umpires are volunteer workers.

8. I shall remember that all officers and other personnel must earn a living and cannot work on Little League full time.

9. I shall offer my services for work whenever possible.

10. I shall encourage my child to follow the Little League Pledge.

—If all parents were to read and follow these promises,

then the games and the season will be more fun for everyone. Posted by Arcadia Little League of Arizona.

Luck. (1) It's better to be lucky than good. (2) A lucky break and an unlucky break will eventually cancel each other out. See also *Rickeyisms* (4).

M

McCarthy's Ten Commandments for Success in Baseball.

1. Nobody ever becomes a ballplayer by walking after a ball.

2. You will never become a .300 hitter unless you take the bat off your shoulder.

3. If what you did yesterday still looks big to you, you haven't done much today.

4. Keep your head up and you may not have to keep it down.

5. When you start to slide, SLIDE. He who changes his mind may have to change a good leg for a bad one.

6. Do not alibi on bad hops. Anybody can field the good ones.

7. Always run them out. You never can tell.

8. Never quit.

9. Do not find too much fault with the umpires. You cannot expect them to be as perfect as you are.

10. A pitcher who hasn't control hasn't anything.

—Joe McCarthy, whose winning percentage as a major-league manager has never been bettered, and his seven World Championships are a record that has only been tied by Casey Stengel. The list was first published in the *Boston Herald* in 1949. It has appeared many places since then, including in *Baseball's Greatest Managers* (1961). This list is often attributed to Philadelphia Athletics star Charles "Chief" Bender.

McGraw's Pendulum. "Every club in a major league race is sure to have a major spurt at some time during the season. Every team is due for a slump at some time during the season." —John J. McGraw, as manager of the New York Giants, in his syndicated column of August 7, 1927.

McKeon's Baseball Philosophy. "Have fun and play loose. I've always believed you let the players play and the coaches coach. You have to give the players the freedom to roam. I don't want robots. I want players who use their imagination out there." —Jack McKeon, after winning the 2003 World Series at age seventy-two after fifty-four years in pro baseball, 3,896 games managing in the minors and majors, and four times being fired. Quoted by Tom Verducci (in *Sports Illustrated*, October 31, 2003), who noted that McKeon was the oldest manager ever to get to the World Series—older than the ground-rule double and the national anthem designation for "The Star-Spangled Banner."

Management. (1) When you ax your manager, replace him with the exact opposite personality. (This has been long posited and is brought up from time to time. In 2002, Richard Griffin of the *Toronto Star* noted that the Blue Jays had gone from Cito Gaston to Tim Johnson, who begat Jim Fregosi, who begat Buck Martinez, who begat Carlos Tosca—all of whom, he suggested, were exact opposites. Richard Griffin, "Managing History for Blue Jays," *Toronto Star,* June 4, 2002.) (2) A team tends to represent the personality of its manager. Low-key management begets a low-key team, and so on. (3) When in doubt, fire the manager. (You can't fire the players, so you fire the manager.) (4) You're hired to be fired. (This is explained by Bob Fowler in the *Orlando Sentinel* [June 25, 1985]: "Owners know that. Managers and players accept the fact. Batboys say they understand, too. Yet when the proverbial ax falls on some team's allegedly unsuspecting 'field general' there is shock." In many cases, the reason for the firing has nothing do with the manager of a team plagued with injuries and underachieving players. Also, it is the rare manager who chooses to leave on his own.) (5) One club's failure is another club's new manager. (6) Within two weeks of being given a vote of confidence by the ownership of a team, the manager is usually gone.

McSherry's Advice to Players. Don't park in the spaces marked "Reserved for Umpires." —The late umpire John McSherry, quoted in the *Chicago Tribune*, April 3, 1994.

Mauch's Math. "It is easier for 25 players to understand one manager than for one manager to understand 25 players." —Baseball legend Gene Mauch, as manager of the Angels.

Murphy's Baseball Law. "Everything that can go amiss during a slump, does." —Rick Braun in the *Milwaukee Journal Sentinel* (May 29, 2007), who elaborated: "During a slump, Murphy's Law will come into effect numerous times. Line drives hit by your team find the opposition's gloves. Weak grounders by the opponent seem to find holes. Scoring opportunities can be dashed simply by having the wrong runner on base at the wrong time."

N

Nevers. (1) Never put the tying or go-ahead run on base. (2) Never get too excited or too disappointed over a young player's performance in spring training or in September. (3) Never suicide squeeze on the first pitch. (4) Never steal when you're two or more runs down. (5) Never throw behind the runner. (6) Never give up a home run on an 0–2 count. (7) Never let the score influence the way you manage. (8) Never give an intentional walk if first base is occupied. (9) Never run yourself out of a big inning. (10) Never break up a pennant winner. —This got a major bit of credence back in the 1930s after the Washington Senators, who won the AL pennant in 1933, traded Goose Goslin to the Tigers and finished seventh the following year. With Goslin in the lineup, Detroit jumped from fifth place in 1933 to first place in 1934. In 1936, Joe McCarthy cited this axiom when he refused to make any deals for Yankee players who had won the pennant. The Yanks won four straight championships, beginning in 1936.

O

Ocker's Observation. "He who puts too much stock in how players perform in March and September is destined to eat fried fungo bat for dinner and munch on soufflé of rosin bag for dessert." —Sheldon Ocker, in the *Akron Beacon Journal* (May 8, 2004), who explained: "During spring training games, some players are trying, others are merely using the at bats and innings on the mound to sharpen their skills. In September, some players on teams with no chance for postseason glory merely go through the motions (look for guys on the field wearing wrist watches)."

October. The reason presidential elections are held in November instead of October is so that they won't conflict with the World Series. —This became a popular bit of baseball lore during the 1948 presidential election year, during which the Cleveland Indians and Harry Truman emerged as victors.

Offense/Defense. (1) If you can't beat them with the lumber, beat them with the leather. (2) Leave your bat in the rack and take your glove to the field. In other words, a hitter should never take his at bats into the field. The offensive game cannot be allowed to affect the defensive game. The converse is also true: a fielder should never take his errors to the plate. (3) A good team makes the other guy commit mistakes.

Old School/New School. "Old-school" baseball—run, throw, catch—versus "new-school" ball—hit, blast, crush.

Olsen's Truisms. (1) Time heals. (2) Hope springs eternal. (3) Bob Uecker is a funny guy. —Drew Olsen, of the *Milwaukee Journal Sentinel,* after the 2002 Brewers franchise-record 106-loss season, during which the club fractured many of baseball's cardinal rules. "Pitchers walked lead-off batters," Olsen explained. "Outfielders missed cutoff men. Too many base runners made the first out of an inning at third base, and the ones who survived were too often stranded by strikeouts."

Owner's Rule of Reality. It is easier to try to change a team's losing ways by firing the manager or general manager than it is by getting rid of the players.

P/Q

Paige's Six Rules for Life (Guaranteed to Bring Anyone to a Happy Old Age). "(1) Avoid fried foods, which angry up the blood. (2) If your stomach disputes you, pacify it with cool thoughts. (3) Keep the juices flowing by jangling around gently as you move. (4) Go very lightly on the vices, such as carrying on in society, as the social ramble ain't restful. (5) Avoid running at all times. (6) Don't look back, something might be gaining on you." —Baseball immortal Satchel Paige. These first appeared in *Collier's* magazine on June 13, 1953, as a sidebar to an article about Paige. It is one of the most famous lists of life rules ever set in print. Despite this, they are often mangled in the requoting. "Don't look behind, something might be catching up with you" is how it appears in one nonbaseball book (*The Rivals: America and Russia Since World War II,* by Adam B. Ulam [1971]). For many years after they appeared, Paige gave out business cards with his rules on the back. When Frank Deford left *Sports Illustrated* after twenty-nine years in 1987, he was asked to write some words of advice. He listed Paige's rules, adding one of his own: (7) Choose your friends in inverse proportion to how seriously they pay attention to the NFL draft. Frank Deford, "Let the Words Wobble; as the Author Leaves SI, He Offers Up a Few Insights," *Sports Illustrated,* May 8, 1989.

Paige's Addenda to the Six Rules. (1) Work like you don't need the money. (2) Love like you've never been hurt.

(3) Dance like nobody's watching. (*Satchel Sez* by David Sterry, Three Rivers Press, 2001.)

Pennock's 10+1 Commandments for Pitchers. (1) Develop your faculty of observation. (2) Conserve your energy. (3) Make contact with players, especially catchers and infielders, and listen to what they have to say. (4) Work everlastingly for control. (5) When you are on the field, always have a baseball in your hand and don't slouch around. Run for a ball. (6) Keep studying the hitters for their weak and strong points. Keep talking with your catchers. (7) Watch your physical condition and your mode of living. (8) Always pitch to the catcher and not the hitter. Keep your eye on that catcher and make him your target before letting the ball go. (9) Find your easiest way to pitch, your most comfortable delivery, and stick to it. (10) Work for what is called a rag arm. A loose arm can pitch overhanded, side arm, three quarter, underhanded, any old way, to suit the situation at hand. —Herb Pennock, nicknamed "the Knight of Kennett Square," pitched in the major leagues from 1912 through 1934. He had a career ERA of 3.60. This legendary list was first published in *Sporting News* during the mid-1940s, and variations have appeared since then, including the eleventh commandment he added to the initial ten before his death in 1948.

In one reprinting of the laws in *Sporting News* (April 24, 1971), Pennock is quoted as saying, "I might give you an eleventh commandment and that is . . . Don't beef at the umpire. Keep pitching with confidence and control of yourself as well as the ball. Don't get it into your head that the umpire is your worst enemy. Fury is as hard on you physically as emotionally."

Piniella's Razor. "If you win wrong, sooner or later you go into a funk. But if you lose right, you have a chance of getting things going in the right direction." —Lou Piniella, as Mariners manager, quoted in the *Seattle Post Intelligencer,* June 4, 1997.

Piniella's Theological Distinction. "My baseball philosophy hasn't changed. I want my teams to play hard and play dirty if they have to. I'm trying to be a better person, but I'm a manager, not a saint." —Lou Piniella, on announcing that he had become a born-again Christian, June 12, 1995.

Pitchers: The Immutable Law of Baseball Physics. Pitchers get hurt, and that's why you can never have enough of them.

Pitching.

1. If you've got the pitching, you've got a chance.

2. You're only as good as your fourth or fifth starter.

3. You can never have enough pitching. Contrary to one of baseball's axioms, there is such a thing as too much pitching, as when two pitchers want the same job: the glamorous if ulcerous assignment of closing relief.

4. The location of pitches matters as much—some say more—than their velocity. In other words, veterans who understand the nuances of pitching are just as important as young galoots who simply bring it.

5. Location beats velocity every time.

6. Momentum is only as good as your next starting pitcher.

7. To have an effective ten-man major-league pitching staff, a team needs ten other pitchers behind it, competing and pushing the big leaguers.

8. The pitchers are ahead of the batters for the first month of the regular season.

9. Pitch for dough, hit for show.

10. You only go as far as your pitching takes you.

11. A starting pitcher must be pretty good to lose twenty games in a season. The logic? A bad

pitcher doesn't get enough chances to lose that many games.

12. Good pitching is contagious.

13. You can only hit what you can see.

14. Good pitchers get better as the game moves along.

15. Starting pitchers should feed off one another. Once one starter hurls a great game, it's up to the next man to live up to the challenge.

16. "Strike one is the best pitch," David Wells noted in August 2004, after a game in which he threw first-pitch strikes to twenty-one of the thirty-one batters he faced.

17. Great pitching beats destiny every time.

18. Good pitching stops good hitting. *Alternatively:* Good pitching beats good hitting, or smart pitching beats good hitting.

—These are some of the most oft-repeated axioms in baseball, but they are also applied elsewhere. Ivan Maisel wrote in his *Sporting News* college football column of January 16, 1995, that this is "a simple axiom of sport that is proved season after season, no matter the sport, no matter the size of the ball. Defense beats offense, good pitching beats good hitting." *Corollary to Axiom 18:* Even truer in September and most true in October. A good pitching staff on the top of its game can dominate a good-hitting club, because to win the game, you have to score runs. A recent example of this was the 2003 ALCS, when the Red Sox showed up with an abundance of good hitters whose bats were controlled by a powerful Yankees pitching staff. Pitching once again beat hitting in a seven-game postseason series, which is when this axiom seems to work best, because a manager who cannot eliminate the weaker bats from his lineup can assign his ace to pitch three games in a seven-game series.

Pitching's Ten Fast Rules. Ten general pitching guides (remembering that no pitching rule is infallible).

1. The guess hitter is that fellow who suddenly looks bad on a pitch that ordinarily doesn't bother him.

2. It takes a while to spot the first-ball hitter, but once he's spotted, he should never be given a good first pitch.

3. The guess hitter is playing percentages, and the more pitches a pitcher can get over the plate, the lower the guess hitter's percentage will be.

4. If a pitcher pitches a hitter by an unvarying formula, the hitter will soon recognize the pattern and set himself for it.

5. The hitter who jumps wildly away from any close pitch is worried about being hit. A pitch that breaks away from him should be effective.

6. A hitter who rocks back on his heels when taking a pitch will probably have trouble with outside pitches.

7. The hitter who chases one pitch outside the strike zone is likely to chase a second.

8. The right-handed batter who's ineffective against a right-hander's curve often gets fat on a left-hander's curve.

9. The lunge hitter (over-strider) will have trouble with a curve or change-up because it's difficult to hit these pitches when the weight is on the front foot.

10. If a hitter looks bad on a pitch (and isn't guessing), that pitch will stick in his mind the rest of the game; therefore, a hurler's other pitches might increase in effectiveness.

—*Baseball Digest,* April 1958.

Plimpton's Correlation. There exists an inverse correlation between the size of the ball and the quality of the writing about the game in which it is used. —The correlation was suggested by the late George Plimpton, who explained: "I have a theory: The larger the ball, the less the writing about the sport. There are superb books about golf, very good books about baseball, not many good books about football, and very few good books about basketball. There are no books about beachballs." It may have first appeared in *Sports Illustrated*, May 10, 1982.

Problem Ballplayers. They learn to say hello when it's time to say good-bye.

Prospects. There is an old baseball axiom that says if you have twenty-five "great" prospects, you'll be lucky if five make the big leagues, three contribute in a major way, and one becomes a star. —Termed "an old baseball axiom" by Kenny Williams, White Sox GM, quoted in the *Daily Herald* (Arlington Heights, Illinois), October 25, 2000.

Pulliam's Injunction. "Take nothing for granted in baseball." —First uttered by Harry Pulliam while president of the National League, circa 1903. By 1908, several signs repeating the motto were posted throughout his office. In 1919, the *New York Times* deemed it the "axiom of the national game." Pulliam helped forge a peace between the American League and the National League that resulted in the National Agreement that governed baseball through 1920.

R

Raper's Rule. "Hit the ball over the fence and you can take your time going around the bases." —John W. Raper, from *What This World Needs* (1945).

Ratios. (1) If you score three runs for every two scored by your opponent, you will win nine games for each four that he wins. If you score four to his three, you will win sixteen games to his nine. (2) Hitting one for three in baseball is considered a radical rate of success.

Reach's Rule. "The secret of happiness is to let the other fellow do the worrying." —A. J. Reach, of baseball and sporting-goods fame, quoted in *Sporting News,* July 28, 1906.

Rickeyisms. (1) It is fatal for a champion to stand pat. (2) Ninety percent of all pitching wildness is above the shoulders. ("I mean mental," the legendary Branch Rickey told a reporter for the *Sporting News* who did not get it.) (3) Addition by subtraction. (One of the most commonly cited Rickeyisms, he applied it to trades, releases, and so on.) (4) Luck is the residue of design. —The most famous and oft-quoted Rickeyism, it was embedded in a longer sentiment: "Things worthwhile generally just don't happen. Luck is a fact, but should not be a factor. Good luck is what is left over after intelligence and effort have combined at their best. Negligence or indifference or inattention are usually reviewed from an unlucky seat. The law of cause and effect and causality both work the same with inexorable exactitudes. Luck is the residue of design." The words were recorded by Arthur Daley in the *New York Times,* November 17, 1965.

Ripken Rule for Youth Baseball. Stop yelling instructions. Let the kids experience competition and the flow of the game. Does a young pianist's teacher sit onstage during recitals? —Cal and Billy Ripken, from their baseball primer *Coaching Youth Baseball the Ripken Way* (2007).

Rule of Three. It takes three. —Steve Warden, *Fort Wayne Journal Gazette,* June 5, 2005. This is a baseball axiom that has been uttered across the ages by every eternal optimist who has worn a glove, hoisted a bat, spit in the dugout, or cried for the home team. From the big leagues to the little, from gray flannels to the legendary White Sox shorts, the hopeful cry of "It takes three" still rings true—no matter how far you are behind, it still takes three outs to finish your half of the ninth inning.

Rules of Thumb. (1) A tie goes to the runner. (2) If you can't make the majors after five years in the minors, it is time to move on. (3) The best team will win two out of every three games, a .666 percentage, and the worst team will lose two out of three, a .333 percentage. —Even the 1962 expansion Mets, with their 40–120 season, won a quarter of their games. Pundit George F. Will weighed in on this rule of thumb in a 1992 article that appeared in the *New York Times:* "Actually the best team will lose more than a third. The average of the best winning percentages in each of the last 25 years is .630. In this sport of the long season, leaving the field just beaten 65 times is excellence."

Rundown Rules. (1) Drive the runner away from the plate or lead base, not toward it, during a rundown play. (2) The defensive player with the ball runs toward the runner.

Ruthian Rules of Thumb. (1) It was more exciting to see the Babe strike out than to see someone else hit a home run. (2) The Ruth is mighty and shall prevail. —Heywood Broun's line after the 1923 World Series (after the Yankees had lost the 1921 and 1922 World Series.)

Ruth's Rules for Training.

1. Always warm up thoroughly before starting to play.
2. Never favor a sore arm. Throw naturally. Most

arm trouble comes from a faulty pitching motion, and then from favoring soreness. Only throw as hard as you can naturally and without pressing.

3. Always keep your arm and body well covered until all sweating has stopped. A slow, thorough rub with a dry towel before bathing is better than a massage to keep muscles supple.

4. Never take a bath until you are entirely through sweating. Keep fully clothed and warm until the sweating has stopped.

5. In bathing take plenty of time and finish up with plenty of cold water; this closes the pores, avoids colds, and prevents stiffness.

6. Never prod, jerk, or punch a sore muscle. No painful or extreme treatment is beneficial unless administered correctly by an expert who knows his business thoroughly.

7. Don't drown in liniments. Keep wool on a sore arm or muscle all the time.

8. Don't drink during a game or for two hours afterward. Leave ice water out entirely. It is very dangerous if taken when you are sweating.

9. Don't eat for two hours before a game.

10. Pitchers should do lots of running and daily leg and body calisthenics. It's the legs that make a pitcher, and these exercises are good not only for endurance but for control and steadiness.

11. Here are some home remedies to remember: A saturated solution of vinegar and water, equal parts, with salt makes an excellent solution for soaking sprains or strains. Also an Epsom salt pack left on all night. Use turpentine on a split or bruised finger after first applying an ice-pack. Zinc ointment always should be used on strawberries or other chafed places. Don't neglect little splits, cuts, blisters, skinned spots, or scrapes. Use antiseptics as soon as possible.

—"A Few Training Rules" appears in *How to Play Baseball*, by Babe Ruth (New York: Cosmopolitan Books, 1931).

Ryan's Rules for Successful Pitching. (1) Keep the leadoff hitter from reaching base. (2) Put the first pitch over for a strike.

—Nolan Ryan, in *Nolan Ryan's Pitcher's Bible* (1991). He adds: "The first pitch doesn't even have to be as good as the others, since many hitters are looking for a ball in a certain zone. If they don't get it, they'll lay off and take a strike."

Saberhagen's Challenge. "Give me 15 runs and airtight defense, and I'll take my chances." —Bret Saberhagen on pitching, quoted by the Associated Press, July 6, 1998.

Scoring. (1) If you do not score, your opponent will. (2) Scoring 252 million runs a game doesn't do you any good if you give up 253 million. (3) After scoring 17 runs—or any other double-digit number over 12—in a game, the team accomplishing that feat will be lucky to score once in the next game.

The Season. (1) The season is a marathon, not a sprint. (2) It really isn't about how you start, but how you finish.

September. (1) Games played early in the season are as important as games played in September. (This was a dictum made popular by Earl Weaver when he managed the Baltimore Orioles.) (2) From Labor Day until the end of the season, the loss column is the one that really counts. —The thinking here is this: The win column can be corrected, because those games have not been played yet and the team that is trailing can still make them up, but the loss column is beyond recall, because those games have already been blown.

Series. Anything can happen in a short series. —Axiom coined by baseball lifers who have seen everything and anything happen in a large number of short series.

Shortstops. (1) No team can be weak at shortstop and still be a contender. (2) Anybody who can play shortstop can play center field.

Simmons's Rule. "A good third base coach can win a dozen or more games a season. And a bad coach can lose that many; except that he doesn't last that long." —Hall of Fame outfielder Al Simmons, who called the job the toughest on the club. "The coach at third gets all the blame when things go wrong and gets none of the credit when things go right." Quoted in an article by Thomas Stinson, "Hot Seat at the Hot Corner—Third Base Coach: In a Little Sand Box in the Grass, He's in Line for All Blame, No Credit," *Atlanta Journal Constitution,* August 27, 1995.

Sliding. Keep your eye on the ball (a cheesy old baseball saying, but in this case, if you want to slide, watching where the ball is makes a lot of sense).

Sparky's Discovery. EACH 24 HOURS, THE WORLD TURNS OVER ON

SOMEONE WHO IS SITTING ON TOP OF IT. —Sign spotted in Detroit manager Sparky Anderson's office in 1984.

Speed. Speed never goes into a slump.

Spring-Training Truisms. (1) No matter how good or how bad a team's standing in the Grapefruit or Cactus League, it is meaningless in terms of the regular season. *Corollary:* Spring-training games don't mean diddly. (2) Never knock in the tying run in the ninth inning of an exhibition game. It is far better to lose than go extra innings in spring training. *Exception:* Nonroster players and those on the bubble are excepted. (3) Never get too excited or too disappointed over a young player's performance in spring training. (4) The pitchers are always ahead of the hitters. (5) As long as you're in camp, you've still got a chance.

Stadium Rule of Thumb. Two million people should live within a twenty-mile radius of the stadium for the franchise to succeed.

Stealing. (1) You can't steal second with one foot on first. (2) If you're not stealing, you're not trying. (3) For a coach or manager, the ability to steal signs is as valuable an asset to a team as a player's ability to steal bases.

Stoppers. The team that has a stopper never comes a cropper.

Streaks. (1) Don't depend on a streak for too long because it will inevitably get taken away. (2) A streak must be respected.

Strikes. "There are times when a club cannot buy a strike."
—Matt Crossman in *Sporting News*, May 21, 2001. He pointed to one team in particular: "The Rangers' starting pitchers couldn't find the strike zone with a compass and a batting tee."

T

Team Behavior. Teammates steer clear of the starting pitcher on game days.

Television. Never take the camera away from the action.
—This is violated from time to time, such as during the 1991 World Series, when CBS was widely criticized for too many bizarre camera angles and too many replays—often at the expense of live action.

Torre's Philosophy.

1. You try to give the player a calm about his play. A sense that you're not going to panic about his game.

2. It takes a lot of work. It's tougher to play this game than it ever has been. Nobody pats you on

the back anymore. If you do well, it's because you are supposed to.

3. But you cannot threaten players. I used to have a lot of rules: You cannot lie out in the sun . . . or swim or play golf. Now my only rule is to make sure you get to the game on time.

4. You have to make yourself available. Don't give anyone an excuse to avoid doing what you want him to do. You have to make sense, give the players a feeling for what you are trying to accomplish.

5. I'm going to win this game. Not because it will give me a better record. But because that is what I was hired to do. I want you to respect that fact. It's my job to make decisions.

—Joe Torre, as manager of the New York Mets in 1977, quoted in *Coach and Athletic Director,* September 2005.

Trades. (1) Better to trade a player one year early rather than one year late. (Advanced by Branch Rickey, among others. Rickey's version: "Trade a player a year too early rather than a year too late.") (2) Some of the best deals are the ones that aren't made. (3) It sometimes takes two years to be able to accurately judge a trade. (4) A player should be traded at the top of his value. (5) When you hurt a rival team with the bat, your trade value goes up with that club. (6) When in doubt, get a pitcher. —The late Jim Murray pointed out back in 1967 that while this was a prevalent belief, it did not always work—Baltimore gave up a pitcher to get Frank Robinson, as did the Cardinals to obtain Orlando Cepeda and Lou Brock. The December 1965 Robinson trade from the Reds was justified by calling him "an old 30." In 1966, his first season with the O's, Robinson won the Triple Crown and was the MVP of the AL and the World Series as Baltimore claimed its first championship. In his six seasons with the O's, Robinson led the team to four World Series. The key player received in the Robinson trade was Milt Pappas, who went 30–29 for the Reds in the two seasons plus he played for the Reds. In the 1970 Series the Reds were beaten in five games by Robinson's Orioles. In 1965, the Cards got Lou Brock in a trade with Chicago that is considered by Cubs fans to be the worst in franchise history. In 1966, the Giants received Ray Sadecki from the Cards in exchange for Cepeda. Sadecki, a proven left-hander, remained a competent pitcher for several more years while Cepeda joined Lou Brock in leading the Cards to back-to-back World Series appearances (1967–1968) and would, like Brock, go on to be elected to the Hall of Fame.

U

Uecker's Advice. "The way to catch a knuckleball is to wait until the ball stops rolling and then pick it up." —Bob Uecker, from his 1982 autobiography *Catcher in the Wry*.

Umpires. (1) Only that which an umpire sees occurs on a ball field. (2) Umpiring is the only profession in which a man must be perfect on Opening Day and improve as the season goes on. (3) A good umpire is an umpire who, when the game is over, is unknown to anybody in the stands.

V

Valentine's Baseball Axiom. "Tomorrow is your best friend." —Bobby Valentine, from a profile entitled "A Bit Out in Left Field—Even for Valentine," by Mike Vaccaro (*Star-Ledger*, August 9, 1999), in which Valentine recalled that this was what he always told minor leaguers in his days as a roving instuctor many years earlier.

Veeck's Distinction. "Next to the confrontation between two highly-trained, finely-honed batteries of lawyers, jungle warfare is a finely-tuned minuet." —Baseball maverick Bill Veeck, in *The Hustler's Handbook* (1965).

Veeck's Law of Enforced Humility. "When you've run as fast as you can up the highest mountain you can find, you will find something or somebody waiting at the top to deflate you." —The late Bill Veeck, from his 1962 book *Veeck as in Wreck.* See also the following entry from the same source.

Veeck's Probe. "I try not to break the rules, but merely to test their elasticity."

Vendor's Vexation. "At the very moment the game gets really tense, the peddlers of hot dogs, season books, beer, pop, popcorn, peanuts, pennants, caps, sun hats, and other items of food, drink, haberdashery, and literature are sent forth in a swarm to obstruct the view." —"A Game for Saints," *Chicago Tribune,* July 30, 1954.

W

Walks. (1) Walks will kill you. (2) You can't defense walks. (3) Nothing hurts pitchers more than walks.

Weaver's Wall Motto. "It's what you learn after you know it all that counts." —Earl Weaver's office wall statement, as quoted by Thomas Boswell in the *Washington Post,* November 25, 1992.

Weinstein's Razor. If you are forty years old and left-handed, you'll be called "crafty." If you are forty years old and right-handed, you'll be called "coach." —Neil Weinstein, June 6, 2001.

Westrum's Dictum. "It's like church. Many attend but few understand." —Wes Westrum in 1962, as a San Francisco Giants coach, on baseball. It is one of the most repeated of all baseball quotations and one used on several occasions in the baseball writing of George F. Will. It has been quoted so often that its original source has been obscured, but if first appeared in the "They Said It" section of *Sports Illustrated* for March 19, 1962.

What's Wrong with Baseball? "What's wrong with baseball is the Yankees." —According to Allen Barra, formerly of the *New York Times* and more recently of the *Wall Street Journal,* this has now become one of baseball's primary axioms, along with "Pitching is 75 percent of the game" and "It ain't over till it's over." This has been the mantra of many since 1921–1923, when the Yankees disproved the old baseball axiom "Pennants cannot be bought."

During that period, in the words of Harold Seymour, baseball's prime historian, "victories were won by teams whose backbone consisted mostly of former Red Sox players masquerading in Yankee uniforms."

Will's Rule. "Baseball is not a game you can play with your teeth clenched." —George F. Will, who made an exception to the rule in the case of Billy Martin, who managed others with "his teeth, fists and soul clenched." The rule first appeared in his column of July 18, 1985.

Wohlford's Baseball Formula. "Ninety percent of this game is half mental." —Milwaukee outfielder Jim Wohlford, quoted in *Sports Illustrated,* October 24, 1977. In an article entitled "Baseball's Mental Game," which appeared in the 2002 edition of the journal *Nine,* anthropologist and former minor leaguer George Gmelch wrote: "In keeping with the sport's mania for quantifying everything, baseball players and coaches often put a number on the mental dimension as a way of stressing its importance. 'Succeeding in pro ball is 90 percent mental. It's big,' said Diamondbacks infielder Andy Fox. 'Baseball is 80 percent mental,' said one manager, 'you have got to make players believe in themselves to perform well.' Or, in the words of former Kansas City outfielder Jim Wohlford, 'Baseball is 90 percent mental half the time.'" Actually, Wohl-ford's Yogi-ism is probably the most accurate of the three, in that some aspects of baseball are more mentally demanding than others.

X/Y/Z

The Yin and Yang of Baseball. As a batter, have a plan when you go to the plate. As a batter, never allow a three-pitch inning. As a pitcher, have a plan when you take the mound. As a pitcher, throw strike one.

Appendix A:

"The Book of Unwritten Baseball Rules," by *Baseball Digest* (1986)

In 1986, *Baseball Digest* published one of the absolute best lists to ever appear about the game of baseball. "The Book of Unwritten Baseball Rules" was a collaborative effort and is quite comprehensive. It had originally appeared in the *Orange County Register* and was put together by Peter Schmuck and Randy Youngman.

1. Never put the tying or go-ahead run on base.
2. Play for the tie at home, go for the victory on the road.
3. Don't hit and run with a 0-2 count.
4. Don't play the infield in early in the game.
5. Never make the first or third out at third.
6. Never steal when you're two or more runs down.
7. Don't steal when you're well ahead.
8. Don't steal third with two outs.

9. Don't bunt for a hit when you need a sacrifice.

10. Never throw behind the runner.

11. Left and right fielders concede everything to center fielder.

12. Never give up a home run on a 0-2 count.

13. Never let the score influence the way you manage.

14. Don't go against the percentages.

15. Take a strike when your club is behind in a ball game.

16. Leadoff hitter must be a base stealer. Designated hitter must be a power hitter.

17. Never give an intentional walk if first base is occupied.

18. With runners in scoring position and first base open, walk the number eight hitter to get to the pitcher.

19. In rundown situations, always run the runner back toward the base from which he came.

20. If you play for one run, that's all you'll get.

21. Don't bunt with a power hitter up.

22. Don't take the bat out of your best hitter's hands by sacrificing in front of him.

23. Only use your bullpen stopper in late-inning situations.

24. Don't use your stopper in a tie game—only when you're ahead.

25. Hit behind the runner at first.

26. If one of your players gets knocked down by a pitch, retaliate.

27. Hit the ball where it's pitched.

28. A manager should remain detached from his players.
29. Never mention a no-hitter while it's in progress.
30. With a right-hander on the mound, don't walk a right-handed hitter to pitch to a left-handed hitter.

Appendix B:

The Unwritten Samurai Code of Conduct for Baseball Players

In his classic work on Japanese baseball, *The Chrysanthemum and the Bat: Baseball Samurai Style* (1983), Robert Whiting listed the following.

ARTICLE 1. The player must be a total team member.

ARTICLE 2. The player must follow established procedure.

ARTICLE 3. The player must undergo hard training.

ARTICLE 4. The player must play "For the team."

ARTICLE 5. The player must demonstrate fighting spirit.

ARTICLE 6. The player must behave like a gentleman on the field.

ARTICLE 7. The player must not be materialistic.

ARTICLE 8. The player must be careful in his comments to the press.

ARTICLE 9. The player must follow the rule of sameness.

ARTICLE 10. The player must behave like a good Japanese off the field.

ARTICLE 11. The player must recognize the team pecking order.

ARTICLE 12. The player must strive for team harmony and unity.

Appendix C:

Bill McGowan's "Don'ts for Umpires" with His Original Comments from His 1949 Textbook, Used at His School for Umpires

1. *Don't take your eye off the ball.* (This is the first rule of baseball and in the long run, one of the most important. Frank Crosetti of the Yankees successfully pulled the hidden ball trick eleven times in two seasons. If you are in the habit of taking your eye off the ball, make certain there isn't a ball player named Crosetti in the park.)

2. *Don't take anything for granted in baseball.* (Never say "I felt sure he would make the catch," or "if he wasn't out, he should have been out." Be positive. Always wait until the play is completed and see it through to the finish.)

3. *Don't call your plays too quickly.* (At first base particularly, take your time. At the last particle of a second a foot off the bag, or a juggled ball, may cause you to reverse yourself, and on this sort of a play the umpire is generally criticized. The players will yell "You always have that thumb in the air"—and plenty more.)

4. *Don't explain your decisions.* (Simply call the plays as you see 'em. That's the best anybody can do. Explaining why you called a runner out or safe in many cases signifies a weakness on the part of the umpire.)

5. *Don't argue with the ball players or managers.* (A manager or player, on a close play, will make a kick. If it is a legitimate protest, listen to their complaint for a brief period. Tell them you called the play as you saw it, and then walk away. When they follow you, you might repeat that it was your judgment. Walk away with a warning finger. If they continue protesting, go through with your threat. Get somebody out of there.)

6. *Don't carry a chip on your shoulder.* (Nothing disturbs a manager or player more than a chesty umpire. When a player tells you a ball was low in a sarcastic manner, reply by saying, "Well, Joe, it looked high enough to me." Suppose you did call one a ball that you later thought you might have called a strike. If the catcher puts up a squawk and raises a rumpus in protesting your decision, under the circumstances, you might possibly say, "It might have been." You will catch more flies with sugar than you will with vinegar.)

7. *Don't look for trouble.* (As far as the "man in blue" is concerned, trouble comes uninvited. For instance, you have called a third strike on a batter; as he walks away from the plate, he grumbles something about your eyesight or your Aunt Kate. Forget it. Umpires make the mistake of yelling "What was that remark?" *That is really looking for trouble.*)

8. *Don't be a grinner.* (It is tactful to smile once in a while on the ball field, but to be out there with a grin on your face almost through an entire game is ridiculous. If you are going to be smiling and grinning most of the game, don't forget the boys are expecting you to keep smiling in those real tough spots. Hence, you are not kidding anyone but yourself.)

9. *Don't challenge ball players.* (Yes, I'll see you under the stands anytime, etc. You know the type. Someday you are going to challenge the wrong guy, "No runs, No hits, No errors.")

10. *Don't talk back to the fans.* (While it is a shame that some of those grandstand managers and grandstand umpires are allowed to get away with so much, still it goes with the job. You have to take a lot of things right on the chin for the good of the game. Pay no attention to the jibes, put cotton in your ears if necessary, but go right on doing your work. After all, those babies are sending the groceries to your home.)

11. *Don't make decisions for your partner.* (The best of us are not too good. It's a tough job at times, and you've got to love it to succeed as an umpire. If shortstop Brown says "Gee, your partner behind the plate has missed a lot of them today,"

ignore the remark. If you ever agree with Mr. Brown you are not an umpire at heart.)

12. *Don't be vindictive.* (No matter how much trouble you have with a team or player today, tomorrow is a new day and a new baseball game. Wipe the slate clean. Never carry a grudge. Remember ball players are fighting to win. They say things on the spur of the moment that they regret an hour later. Better than 95 percent of the players with whom I've had run-ins have later apologized in their own way.)

13. *Don't let coaches call your plays.* (Speak to them in a nice way about it. Don't be sarcastic. Inject a little humor with your warning if you wish. He knows the golden rule. Earle Combs is as fine a gentleman as you'll ever meet. Once in a while he becomes excited, and with palms downward will signal a runner [naturally, a Yankee] is safe. I always manage to get a laugh, and at the same time an apology from the former great ball player by saying something to this effect: "You will be on our staff next year, Earle, if you keep improving on those close decisions!")

14. *Don't take your eyes off the pitcher once he steps on that rubber.* (The very moment you turn your head for the first time during a game, that's the time a pitcher will make a false move and the opposing team swarms on the field, crying, "Balk! Balk! Balk!" Well, if you've never been in hot water, this will be the turning point.)

15. *Don't clown on the field.* (No matter what a player has done to draw a laugh, stay out of the picture if you happen to be

wearing a blue suit and carrying an umpire's indicator. Umpires are hired to render decisions in baseball—without a doubt the greatest game on God's green earth. If you are a comedian on the field, I strongly advise taking up show business. They will surely take care of you, providing you have the goods.)

16. *Don't turn away from a play too quickly.* (Something may happen. On an attempted double play, the second baseman may fail to tag the bag with his foot; he may drop the ball before he gets a firm hold on it, or he may drop the ball in the act of throwing it to first base, which under the rules is not construed as a dropped ball. I repeat . . . take nothing for granted in baseball—wait until the play is completed at second base before turning your head.)

17. *Don't attract too much attention.* (It's all right to have a little color. Hustle your head off! Move around! Be alert! Be alive! Concentrate on every pitched ball regardless of whether you are behind the plate or on the bases. If you are going to wave out a runner who is out by fifteen feet with a great demonstration of arm motion, make sure you go through the same gestures when the going is toughest. The boys who toss that little white pill around will love you for that.)

18. *Don't work without proper equipment.* (Make sure you are well protected from all possible injuries. A foul tip could ruin an umpire's career and possibly his life.)

19. *Don't hold idle conversations with players or coaches.* (Anybody can talk a good game. It is the umpire who umpires a good

game who goes up the ladder. Besides, after listening to your chatter, the coach or player invariably goes back to the bench and remarks, "What a barber that guy is.")

20. *Don't stand on a dime.* (Try to be a step ahead of the players on every play. Be on top of your plays. Keep the ball game moving by hustling the players but keep hustling yourself.)

21. *Don't call your plays on the run.* (Hustle over to a base on a play—take up a stationary position when giving your decision. But get over to the right spot in a hurry.)

22. *Don't fail to call interference plays immediately.* (When you call a runner out for running more than three feet from a direct line to avoid being touched by the ball in the hands of a fielder, call it quickly and don't keep it a secret. You will be in a predicament if you wait for a team to protest and then decide the runner ran out of line. *BEAT 'EM ALL TO THE PUNCH.*)

23. *Don't fail to expect the unexpected.* (Figure out plays in advance. What might happen? What could happen? Keep your head out of the stands. Regardless of the score, stay in that ball game.)

24. *Don't forget you represent America's National Game.* (This goes for on and off the ball field. Remember, despite the jibes, the mob scenes, or the unkind things they say about the "Boys in Blue," despite the thankless job it is, all umpires are proud to the core of their jobs and their 100 years' record for honesty and integrity.)

25. *Don't kid yourself.* (And I'll leave that one to you.)

Bibliography

Allen, Ethan. *Baseball: Major League Technique and Tactics.* New York: Macmillan, 1953.

———. *Baseball Play and Strategy.* New York: Ronald Press, 1953.

———. *Baseball Techniques Illustrated.* New York: A. S. Barnes, 1951.

Allen, Lee. *The Hot Stove League.* New York: A. S. Barnes, 1955.

Araton, Harvey. "Palmeiro, and Baseball, Chose Not to Follow the Way Paved by Ripken." *New York Times,* August 12, 2005.

Asinof, Eliot. "New Yankee Manager Dallas Green on the Spot." *New York Times,* March 26, 1989.

Associated Press. "Court: Calif. Athlete Can't Sue Over 'Beanball' Pitch." *Community College Week,* April 24, 2006.

Beene, Darin. "Griffey's Return a Thumbs-Up." *Tacoma News Tribune,* June 23, 2007.

Bench, Johnny. *The Complete Idiot's Guide to Baseball.* New York: Alpha Books, 1999.

BIBLIOGRAPHY

Bernstein, Ross. *The Code: Baseball's Unwritten Rules and Its Ignore-at-Your-Own-Risk Code of Conduct.* Chicago: Triumph Books, 2008.

Bolender, Derek. "MLB: Unwritten Rules, Steroids, and Consequences." Bleacher Report, February 20. 2008. Available at www.bleacherreport.com.

Boswell, Thomas. "For a Coach and a Struggling Team, You Can't Beat Character." *Washington Post,* November 25, 1992.

———. "Some Players Peak Early, and Some Never Do." *Washington Post,* May 16, 2002.

Bouton, Jim. *Ball Four.* New York: World Publishing, 1970.

Buck, Ray. "A Look at Game's Unwritten Rules." *Boston Globe,* October 25, 2004.

Canseco, Jose. *Juiced: Wild Times, Rampant 'Roids, Smash Hits, and How Baseball Got Big.* New York: Reganbooks/HarperCollins, 2005.

Cart, Julie. "In Pitching, Applied Science More Like Applied Substance." *Los Angeles Times,* October 17, 1991.

Chass, Murray. "Bats in The Bronx: A Yankee Caper." *New York Times,* June 17, 1990.

Cobb, Ty, with Al Stump. *My Life in Baseball: The True Record.* Lincoln: University of Nebraska Press, 1993.

Cochrane, Gordon S. "Mickey." *Baseball: The Fan's Game.* New York: Funk and Wagnalls, 1939.

Coffin, Tristram Potter. *The Old Ball Game: Baseball in Folklore and Fiction.* New York: Herder and Herder, 1971.

Condon, David. "In the Wake of the News." *Chicago Daily News,* October 21, 1963.

Considine, Bob. "The Line: The Dodgers, Cobb, Lesnevich." *Washington Post.* August 28, 1941.

Couch, Greg. "Stealing Signs: Fair or Foul? Baseball's On-Field Intelligence Gathering Has Been Going On Since the Early Years of the Major Leagues." *Baseball Digest*, August 2002.

Daley, Arthur. "Controversial No-Hitter." *New York Times*, May 24, 1959.

———. "Finis for the Chief?" *New York Times*, November 4, 1954.

Deane, Bill. "The Treatment." *Baseball Digest*, November 2003.

Dickson, Paul. *The Hidden Language of Baseball*. New York: Walker, 2003.

Eskenazi, Gerald. *A Sportwriter's Life*. Columbia: University of Missouri Press, 2004.

Fallon, Brian E. "Unwritten Rules? Baseball's Code of Conduct Is Blurring." *Washington Times*, June 25, 2002.

Fitzpatrick, Tom. "McSherry Calls It—Ump's Life Not So Bad." *Chicago Sun-Times*, July 28, 1986.

Fraley, Gerry. "Managers Vs. Umpires: Throughout Baseball History, Team Pilots and Men in Blue Have Failed to Mix: Interpreting the Many Rules That Can Change the Outcome of a Game Often Keeps Skippers and Arbiters at Odds." *Baseball Digest*, September 2007.

Fullerton, Hugh S. "The Baseball Primer." *American Magazine*, June 1912.

Garagiola, Joe. *Baseball Is a Funny Game*. New York: Bantam, 1960.

Glanville, Doug. "Lovers, Not Fighters." *New York Times*, May 25, 2008.

Gmelch, George. "Baseball's Mental Game." *Nine*, 2000.

Goode, Erica. "To Yankee Second Baseman, Throwing Is No Idle Thought." *New York Times*, June 17, 2000.

Gutman, Dan. *It Ain't Cheatin' If You Don't Get Caught*. New York: Penguin, 1990.

Hample, Zack. *Watching Baseball Smarter*. New York: Vintage, 2007.

Harber, Paul. "Chasing the Dream of Playing Big-League Ball: Veterans Offer Survival Guide for Local Players." *Boston Globe*, June 29, 2003.

Harper, Lucius C. "Dustin' Off the News: Baseball Pauses to Honor Heroes; No Black Ones." *Chicago Defender,* March 11, 1939.

Haudricourt, Tom. "Playing by the Rules That Are Not in Book." *Milwaukee Journal Sentinel,* August 2, 2001.

Holtz, Randy. "Fair or Foul? Unwritten Rules Always in Play: Regarding A-Rod Episode, Rockies Mindful of 'Code.'" *Rocky Mountain News,* June 21, 2007.

Holtzman, Jerome. *No Cheering in the Press Box.* New York: Holt, Rinehart & Winston, 1974.

Honig, Donald. *The Man in the Dugout: Fifteen Big League Managers Speak Their Minds.* Lincoln: University of Nebraska Press, 1993.

Hornig, Doug. *The Boys of October.* New York: McGraw-Hill, 2004.

Hornsby, Rogers. *My Kind of Baseball.* New York: McKay, 1953.

Hornsby, Rogers, and Bill Surface. *My War with Baseball.* New York: Coward-McCann, 1962.

———. "You've Got to Cheat to Win in Baseball." *True,* August 1961.

Hruby, Patrick. "Basebrawl Etiquette." *Insight on the News,* June 19, 2000.

Hutchens, John K. "The Man Who Is Never Out: He Is the Baseball Umpire. But His Job Is Not Just to 'Call Them Fast and Walk Away Tough.'" *New York Times,* September 5, 1943.

James, Bill. *The Bill James Guide to Baseball Managers from 1870 to Today.* New York: Scribner, 1997.

Jones, Jennifer. "Unwritten Baseball: The Game's Etiquette Is a Nebulous Subject." *Chicago Sun-Times,* May 27, 2005.

Jones, Todd. "Blue Laws." *Sporting News,* May 14, 2001.

———. "It's Not Written That a New Teammate Has to Share Inside Info—and He Usually Doesn't." *Sporting News,* July 15, 2005.

———. "There Is a Thin Line between Doctoring and Cheating." *Birmingham News,* June 19, 2005.

———. "Unwritten Rules Are Not Meant to Be Broken." *Sporting News,* June 11, 2001.

———. "Unwritten Rules Often Trump Official Line." *Birmingham News,* July 3, 2005.

Jordan, Pat. "The Hardest Stuff." *New York Times Magazine,* September 14, 2003.

Kelly, Kevin. "Unwritten Rules." *St. Petersburg Times,* August 12, 2001.

Kennedy, Kostya. "His Memory Is Perfect." *Sports Illustrated,* October 14, 1996.

Kermisch, Al. "Bucky Harris and Walter Johnson Ignored 'Unwritten Rules' on No-Hit Games—from a Researcher's Notebook." *Baseball Research Journal,* 2001.

Kieran, John. "Sports of the Times: The Illustrious Robert M. Grove. Looking Over the Record. Stubborn Connie Mack. Taming Down. Irrelevant Details." *New York Times,* August 21, 1931.

Koppett, Leonard. *The New Thinking Man's Guide to Baseball.* New York: Fireside, 1991.

———. "Seaver Mixes Up Pitches." *New York Times,* June 12, 1975.

Kroichick, Ron. "Baseball's Unwritten Code of Ethics: Conduct Governed by Rules Based on Respecting the Game." *San Francisco Chronicle,* May 12, 2000.

Kurkjian, Tim. "Sign Language." *Sports Illustrated,* July 27, 1997.

Lewin, Josh. "Announcers Have Their Own Code." *Sporting News,* July 15, 2005.

Lindquist, Carl. "High in the Catbird Seat Sits Barber, a Vet of 33 Seasons at Mike." *Sporting News,* May 7, 1966.

Lowitt, Bruce. "Larsen Brings Word 'Perfect' to Series." *St. Petersburg Times,* November 22, 1999.

Luke, Bob. *Dean of Umpires: Bill McGowan.* Jefferson, N.C.: McFarland, 2005.

McGraw, John J. "McGraw Says Giants Are Feared." *Washington Post,* August 7, 1927.

Mack, Connie. *Connie Mack's Baseball Book.* New York: Knopf, 1950.

———. *My 66 Years in the Big Leagues.* Philadelphia: John C. Winston, 1950.

McKee, Mike. "California Supreme Court: Ballplayer May Not Sue over Bean Ball." *Legal Intelligencer,* April 11, 2006.

"A Manager for All Seasons: Joe Torre Gets the Most out of His Workers, Makes His Boss Happy, and Delivers Wins. He May Be the Model for Today's Corporate Managers. And He's Not Afraid to Cry." *Fortune,* April 30, 2001.

Mathewson, Christy. *Pitching In a Pinch; or, Baseball from the Inside.* New York: G. P. Putnam's Sons, 1912.

Mays, Willie, with Howard Liss. *My Secrets of Playing Baseball.* New York: Viking Press, 1967.

Mead, William. *The Inside Game: Baseball's Master Strategists.* Alexandria, Va.: Redefinition, 1991.

Monteleone, John J., ed. *Branch Rickey's Little Blue Book: Wit and Strategy from Baseball's Last Wise Man.* New York: Macmillan, 1995.

Morgan, Joe, with Richard Lally. *Baseball for Dummies.* Foster City, Calif.: IDG Books Worldwide, 1998.

Ocker, Sheldon. "It's Time for Westbrook." *Akron Beacon Journal,* May 8, 2004.

Okrant, Daniel. *Nine Innings.* New York: Ticknor & Fields, 1985.

Peterson, Ivars. "Quantum Baseball: A Baseball Analogy Illuminates a Paradox of Quantum Mechanics." *Science News,* August 5, 1989.

Povich, Shirley. "This Morning." *Washington Post,* March 19, 1936, May 2, 1939, January 25, 1962, December 18, 1966, July 13, 1996.

Queenan, Bob. "How Far Can Players Go? Don't Get Personal, Umps Say." *Cincinnati Post,* August 9, 1991.

Rumill, Ed. "Monbouquette's Pride Factor in No-Hitter; One Reached." *Christian Science Monitor,* August 2, 1982.

Ruth, George Herman. *Babe Ruth's Own Book of Baseball.* New York: G. P. Putnam, 1928.

Ryan, Nolan, and Tom House, with Jim Rosenthal. *Nolan Ryan's Pitcher's Bible.* New York: Simon & Schuster, 1991.

Schulman, Henry. "Stumped Giants Fall to Phillies." *San Francisco Chronicle,* August 2, 2002.

Schwarz, Alan. "In the Postseason, Velocity Is Destiny." *New York Times,* October 1, 2006.

———. *The Numbers Game: Baseball's Lifelong Fascination with Statistics.* New York: Thomas Dunne, 2004.

Seymour, Harold. *Baseball: The Golden Age.* New York: Oxford University Press, 1989.

Silver, Marc. "Play Ball!" *U.S. News & World Report,* April 19, 2004.

Smith, H. Allen. *Let the Crabgrass Grow.* New York: Bernard Geis, 1960.

Stone, Larry. "Home Runs Reason to Stargaze; Unlike the Past, Players Admiring Their Spectacle." *Houston Chronicle,* August 22, 2004.

———. "No Staying Quiet during a No-Hitter." *Seattle Times,* April 13, 2007.

Sullivan, Jerry. "Time to Erase Baseball's Code of Conduct." *Buffalo News,* August 8, 2001.

Sullivan, Paul. "Auribe's Ploy Inspires Foul Mood: Stop Sign at Second Base Fools Lee, Angers Baker." *Chicago Tribune,* May 22, 2005.

Thorn, John, and Pete Palmer. *The Hidden Game of Baseball.* New York: Doubleday, 1985.

Torre, Joe. "Coaching Philosophy." *Coach and Athletic Director,* September 2005.

Treder, Steve. "The Persistent Color Line: Specific Instances of Racial Preference in Major League Player Evaluation Decisions after 1947." *Nine* 10, no. 1 (2001).

Veeck, Bill. *Veeck as In Wreck.* New York: Putnam, 1962.

Verducci, Tom. "What Is Rickey Henderson Doing in Newark? The Greatest Leadoff Hitter of All Time Is Beating the Bushes, Trying to Get Back to the Majors—and Still Leaving 'Em Laughing at Every Stop." *Sports Illustrated,* June 23, 2003.

Vestal, Peter. "A License to Bean? 'Avila' Broadens Primary Assumption of Risk Doctrine." *Recorder,* November 8, 2006.

Wendel, Tim. *The New Face of Baseball: The One-Hundred-Year Rise and Triumph of Latinos in America's Favorite Sport.* New York: HarperCollins, 2003.

White, Paul. "Why Is Peeking Such a Sin?" *USA Today Baseball Weekly,* June 16, 1993.

Will, George F. *Men at Work: The Craft of Baseball.* New York: Macmillan, 1990.

———. "Paranoid in Pinstripes." *New York Times,* April 5, 1992.

———. "A Season Spoiled." *Washington Post,* February 8, 2001.

Williams, Ted. *The Science of Hitting.* New York: Simon & Schuster, 1970.

Wills, Maury, with Don Freeman. *How to Steal a Pennant.* New York: Putnam, 1976.

Winfield, Dave. *The Complete Baseball Player.* New York: Avon, 1990.

Young, Fay. "Through the Years: Who Knew Not When to Die." *Chicago Defender,* May 15, 1943.

Acknowledgments

I began working on this book in March 2001 while on assignment for an article on the unwritten rules for Major League Baseball's World Series program. The interviews for this book were conducted intermittently since then, many during three extended reporting visits to the Grapefruit and Cactus leagues.

I would like to thank the following managers, coaches, and players for their time: Yogi Berra, Mike Bordick, Larry Bowa, Terry Bevington, George Brett, Dave Clark, Terry Crowley, Rich Dauer, Rick Dempsey, Larry Dierker, Mike Easler, Jim Evans, Tom Gamboa, Dallas Green, Greg Gross, Mike Hargrove, Billy Hatcher, the late Elrod Hendricks, Reggie Jackson, Todd Jones, Lamar Johnson, Tony La Russa,

Charlie Manuel, Buck Martinez, Don Mattingly, John Mizerock, Mickey Morandini, Tony Muser, Tim Naehring, Jerry Narron, Sam Perlozzo, Alonzo Powell, Mickey Rivers, Leon Roberts, Bill Robinson, Tommy Sandt, Bob Schaefer, Bruce Tanner, the late Syd Thrift, Jeff Torborg, Joe Torre, John Vukovich, and Don Zimmer.

A number of writers who cover the baseball beat have helped me. Leading off this list is Tim Kurkjian of ESPN, who encouraged me to write this book. Others include Bill Livingston of the *Cleveland Plain Dealer,* Mark McGuire of the *Albany Times Union,* Dave Scheiber of the *St. Petersburg Times,* and Peter Schmuck, former president of the Baseball Writers Association of America and baseball writer for the *Baltimore Sun.*

I would also like to thank a group of friends and associates who have helped me collect information and find leads, and otherwise acted as friends of this project: Dave Kelly and Tom Mann at the Library of Congress; Timothy J. Wiles, director of research, and his staff at the National Baseball Hall of Fame Library; and Dave Kaplan, director of the Yogi Berra Museum & Learning Center.

Baseball writers, broadcasters, and researchers affiliated with SABR (the Society for American Baseball Research) who shared their notes and thoughts on this subject include David

W. Anderson, Roger Angell, Priscilla Astifan, Darryl Brock, Bill Deane, Dan Gutman, Zack Hample, Ted Hathaway, John Holway, Paul Hunkele, Kevin P. Kerr, Howard Kleinberg, Bob Luke, Norman Macht, Fred Manfra, Skip McAfee, Dick McBane, Andy McCue, Joe McGillen, William B. Mead, Ron Menchine, Ed Michaels, Peter Morris, Buster Olney, Bill Plummer III, Dave Smith, Dan Gutman, Dan Shaughnessy, Willie Weinbaum, and Paul Wendt.

Special thanks and appreciation to agent Ron Goldfarb, for placing this project; to Skip McAfee, for his many hours of help; and to Bill Young, to whom the book is dedicated.